Day by Day with God

ROOTING WOMEN'S LIVES IN THE BIBLE

MAY–AUGUST 2010

Christina Press
BRF
Tunbridge Wells/Abingdon

The Bible Reading Fellowship,
15 The Chambers, Vineyard, Abingdon OX14 3FE

First published in Great Britain 2010

ISBN 978 1 84101 555 2

Distributed in Australia by:
Willow Connection, PO Box 288, Brookvale, NSW 2100.
Tel: 02 9948 3957; Fax: 02 9948 8153;
E-mail: info@willowconnection.com.au

Distributed in New Zealand by:
Scripture Union Wholesale, PO Box 760, Wellington
Tel: 04 385 0421; Fax: 04 384 3990;
E-mail: suwholesale@clear.net.nz

Acknowledgments

Contents

Contributors

Alie Stibbe works as the Planning Officer at West Herts College. She is also a freelance writer and mother of four. She is married to Mark Stibbe, Director of The Father's House Trust: www.thefathershousetrust.com

Tracy Williamson, an author and speaker, is part of Marilyn Baker Ministries, bringing a message of hope and assurance of God's love through Marilyn's music and her own testimony, insights and teaching seminars.

Margaret Killingray works for the London Institute for Contemporary Christianity. She is a Reader in the diocese of Rochester and is married to a retired history professor.

Rosemary Green is active in her local church, in which she leads a pastoral care team. Her family of four offspring and 14 (mostly young) grandchildren are scattered around the UK

Chris Leonard lives in Surrey with her husband, both 20-something offspring having fled the nest. With 17 books published, Chris leads many creative writing holidays and workshops. See www.chris-leonard-writing.co.uk

Ali Herbert leads the women's ministry *Girlzone* at St Mary's, London, plays in the band Pastiche and is married to Nick. They have two (mostly!) delightful children, Gracie and Josiah.

Diana Archer is a writer, mum of three, and wife of Graham, an Anglican vicar in Southampton. She wrote *Who'd Plant a Church*, a warts-and-all account of church planting in the UK. She is passionate about words, chocolate and the extraordinary truth of the gospel.

Fiona Barnard is a staff member of Friends International. Her principal work is among international students, encouraging local Christians to reach out in friendship to those temporarily far from home.

Sandra Wheatley's life changed abruptly in 1987 when she was diagnosed with MS. Unable to continue her nursing career, her life is nonetheless lived to the full as she seeks to know God and make him known through the struggles and 'delights' of living with a progressive disability.

Catherine Butcher writes...

What on earth are you doing? Do you ever pause to ask yourself what you were created to do? You might have asked such questions when you were in your teens—when life seemed to present different choices. But have you asked yourself recently, 'What am I here for? What task has God given me to do? What is God saying to me today?'

Some people would like a detailed life-plan written on tablets of stone. They seem to suggest that God wants to give comprehensive instructions for every minor decision. Others feel that God couldn't possibly want them for any purpose—and he certainly wouldn't be interested in giving them detailed instructions.

Certainly there are times when God's plans are meticulously laid and we need to listen and obey. Most of the time, we are to follow God's priorities: loving him and loving our neighbour—working as part of Christ's body to establish his kingdom. All of the time, God's Holy Spirit is whispering to us, reminding us what Jesus has said, what his priories are, and what his plans are.

We look forward to the day when we shall see him 'face to face', when what we now know only in part will be fully revealed to us. For now, we are part of Christ's body—together, showing the world what God is like.

As you work alongside other parts of Christ's body—people from other church traditions—do you expect to learn from them as you work together? You might find it difficult to work with people who worship differently or who understand faith differently. You might even think they are completely wrong. But God, in his wisdom, has revealed different facets of himself in different ways. We need to listen and learn from each other to see a bigger picture of who God is and what he wants to do.

Over the next four months, as you use *Day by Day with God* and think about your identity as a child of God and what God calls you to do with your time, take to heart these words from Hebrews 10:24–25: 'Let us consider how we may spur one another on towards love and good deeds. Let us not give up meeting together, as some are in the habit of doing, but let us encourage one another—and all the more as you see the Day approaching.'

Worry and anxiety

'But seek first his kingdom and his righteousness, and all these things will be given to you as well. Therefore do not worry about tomorrow, for tomorrow will worry about itself. Each day has enough trouble of its own.'

In spring 2008 my husband announced to the Annual Meeting of St Andrew's church that he was highly unlikely to be the vicar of the church in twelve months' time. It's very unusual for someone in the Anglican ministry to give such an extended period of notice but, once it was said, there was no going back. For a long time my husband had wanted to focus on bringing the message of the Father-heart of God to those who needed to hear it, and it was becoming increasingly difficult for him to do this and to minister in a very large, busy church. A decision had to be made, so we decided it was time to leave the security of the institution and follow God's call out into the big wide world.

As you can imagine, with four children still at home and living in a vicarage that did not belong to us, there was a lot that needed to fall into place before we could make the leap. The potential for worrying about 'tomorrow' was enormous, and I am a worrier: I literally tear my hair out. My main worry was 'Where are we going to live?' closely followed by 'How are we going to afford to live?' and many lesser niggles.

In the end I had to remind myself that Jesus had said that worrying would not add a single hour to our lives. In fact, it would probably do the reverse. I could easily have lost all my hair and worried myself to death over the whole issue, so finally I decided that the only thing to do was to face each day hand in hand with the Lord and learn something about dealing with anxiety along the way.

....

Lord, when I am faced with seemingly insurmountable situations, help me remember that worry will not solve anything. Make me stand still and turn my face to you.

AHS

Somewhere to live?

The fruit of righteousness will be peace; the effect of righteousness will be quietness and confidence for ever. My people will live in peaceful dwelling places, in secure homes, in undisturbed places of rest.

As I've said, when my husband told me that God was calling him out of the local church ministry, my main worry was 'Where are we going to live?' All our married life we had lived in church accommodation and I couldn't imagine doing anything different until we were forced to retire.

Regarding retirement, I had practised Proverbs 30:24–25 (about the small, wise ant that stores up food while it's summer), being as entrepreneurial as I could, saving every penny so we would not end up in a charity-aided flat for the 'distressed clergy'. Despite my efforts, I knew that my achievements were insufficient to meet the practical requirements of being called out of the vicarage 20 years too soon. But isn't that a wonderful picture of God's grace? We can never work hard enough or contribute enough to put ourselves in the place, physical or spiritual, that God wants us to be. Only he himself can do that, through the amazing riches of his grace (Ephesians 1:7).

Holding on to that knowledge, I went out obediently to look for a house that would meet our needs. I almost prayed that I'd find nothing or, if I did find something, that it would be financially impossible and we could stay put. Unsurprisingly I discovered that the Lord had gone ahead of me. He directed my steps to a modest house that was perfectly suited, not only to our needs but also our unspoken hopes (Ephesians 3:20). National economic downturn can be a blessing! Now we have an 'undisturbed place of rest'. I'm not sure it has been due to my righteousness (v. 17)—maybe my obedience—but it has shown me that if we seek first his kingdom, everything else really will be added to us according to our needs.

....

Thank you, Lord, that you go ahead of us in the large and small concerns of life and provide all we need to do your will. Help us to trust you.

AHS

A word in season

'When you are brought before synagogues, rulers and authorities, do not worry about how you will defend yourselves or what you will say, for the Holy Spirit will teach you at that time what you should say.'

When one aspect of your life begins to change, so does everything else. At the time when I was coming to terms with having to leave the vicarage, I was also working part-time as an administrator in one town and had another temporary three-day-a-week job in another. Being a practical person, I realised that if Mark was going to make the leap into a freelance occupation, then I needed a 'proper' job to make sure there was some regular income, however small. So I was looking not only for a house but also for a job. The house needed to be not only near the town where Mark felt he was called to be based, but also near a railway station in case I had to travel into London every day. I had only the vaguest idea of what kind of job I could do and had my mind fixated on London, not thinking that anything suitable could turn up nearer to 'home'.

How wrong I was! Just as the house hunting began to look up, I was asked to consider applying for an opening at the place where I worked in that same town. On paper there was no way I would have given the job a second look if I hadn't already been working there: it looked too challenging. As it turned out, I had a London-based interview that was a total flop, but the local interview went really well. I know going for a job interview is not quite the same as being dragged before a synagogue to defend your faith, but, if the Lord wants you in a certain place, he certainly gives you the words and answers to get you where he wants you to be.

....

Lord, in the anxious situations I meet, speak to me and put words in my mouth. As you did for Moses, help me speak and teach me what to do (Exodus 4:15).

AHS

Calm after the storm

When I said, 'My foot is slipping,' your love, O Lord, supported me.
When anxiety was great within me, your consolation brought joy to
my soul.

As I was about to change my two part-time jobs (one temporary) for
a permanent full-time job, we were also about to pass the point of no
return in committing ourselves to the house that we believed was to
be ours. This was a crisis point for me personally. It is all very well
theorising about making a big move and sacrificing your perceived
security to follow God's call into the unknown but, when reality
begins to bite, it is a whole different situation.

Taking the full-time job was not a problem—I would have done
that anyway—but signing on the line for a property was a massive
step. The thought of it completely freaked me out. That was when my
'enemies' rose up to confront me—not people, but the fears, worries,
doubts, even panic of not being in total control of a situation, and
being on the verge of taking the biggest risk of my life next to getting
married. At that point, I really had a go at my husband about whether
he'd actually heard God right. I was especially nervous as, recently,
I and several people I knew had experienced situations in which we
had thought God was calling us to something—backed up with
words of knowledge from others—only to find that these 'callings'
had just been castles in the air. My 'foot was slipping' indeed and I
was very anxious—until the situation was solved.

I like the thought of the Lord's 'consolation' mentioned in Psalm
94. It gives me the feeling of being comforted in the midst of circumstances that can't be changed—because I recognise that the circumstances will be for my own blessing in the long run.

....

*Lord, when I am beside myself, be there beside me, too. I have no
one else to support me. Amen*

AHS

Fat and frantic?

'Therefore I tell you, do not worry about your life, what you will eat or drink; or about your body, what you will wear. Is not life more important than food, and the body more important than clothes?'

When I worry, not only do I tear my hair out; I also eat. I wish I was one of those people who lose their appetite when they worry, but I am the complete opposite. Despite a successful diet in the spring, the thought of leaving the security of the vicarage caused me to slip back into eating badly. This was compounded by the sudden unexpected rise in food prices that summer. Some healthy foods doubled in price and my scrooge-like mentality meant that these items dropped off the shopping list, to be replaced by cheaper alternatives that were not good for the waistline.

I began to put on weight as I was eating more and eating the wrong food. I then began to worry because the outfits I had invested in for work began to feel tight, and I couldn't afford a bigger size. That in turn caused me to worry that if we couldn't afford to eat and clothe ourselves when we were living in provided accommodation, how would we manage to feed and clothe ourselves when we had a hefty mortgage to pay? I hadn't a clue.

I can hear you saying, 'Where is your faith, woman? Where is your self-discipline?' At the time, they were nowhere. I know that life is more important than food and clothes but, looking back, I realise that 25 years in a vicarage had caused to me lose sight of 'life': I was just surviving. Twelve months later, I find that I am grabbing back life with both hands. Our food bill and our weight have decreased and the saving has provided some new clothes.

Life is the most important thing: it is so easy to lose sight of life when we are worn down over a period of time or face a sudden crisis.

....

Lord, when I can't see the wood for the trees, lead me out of the thicket into a spacious place where I can breathe in life in all its fullness.

AHS

Age is a state of mind

So then, banish anxiety from your heart and cast off the troubles of your body, for youth and vigour are meaningless.

I know they say we get older and wiser—but I am also getting older and wider. I expect many of us share a common consternation at what we see in the mirror each morning, in fact, I try not to look too often, except to make sure there are no stray hairs sticking out of my chin! It also doesn't help having a very beautiful 20-year-old daughter in the house. Barring the changes in fashion and body ornamentation that have taken place over the last 28 years, looking at my daughter reminds me of how I used to be: in fact, I was slimmer at her age than she was at age 11.

Dwelling on that thought for too long can provoke the subconscious sense of grief that all women feel when they recognise that their youthfulness is receding rapidly into the distance. Allowing that sense of grief to take root in our lives can produce the anxiety of the heart mentioned in today's verses—especially if we are so busy thinking about our lost youth that we lose our footing coming down a flight of steps in a pair of shoes with less-than-sensible heels.

Nevertheless, today's verses encourage us to understand that youth and vigour are meaningless. Why? Because as we get older, we become more at home with who we are and what is important in life. I wholly support Rosemary Conley's comment that 'getting older is fab… you have more wisdom, a better balance of what's important, and you've learnt to say "no"—I wouldn't swap my place for anybody's.' Adding that realisation to a deep, mature faith in Christ truly makes us into women who can 'laugh at the days to come' (Proverbs 31:25).

....

Lord, help me remember you do not look at the things we think are important, but that you look at the heart (1 Samuel 16:7). Help me adjust my priorities accordingly. Amen

AHS

Right concerns

An unmarried woman or virgin is concerned about the Lord's affairs: her aim is to be devoted to the Lord in both body and spirit. But a married woman is concerned about the affairs of this world—how she can please her husband.

There are many people who find Paul's words in 1 Corinthians 7 challenging, if not downright difficult. Two hundred years ago, verse 20 ('Each one should remain in the situation which he was in when God called him') was used by the aristocratic clergy to keep the peasant population in its place across much of northern Europe. This attitude became such a part of the cultural mindset that many modern Westerners have difficulty believing that they can achieve anything in life—in great contrast with Paul's exhortation in Philippians 4:13 to believe 'I can do everything through him who gives me strength.'

Never does the idea of 'remaining in your situation' get so complicated as when it is tangled up with Paul's thoughts on marriage—especially verse 34 in today's reading. For a wife, pleasing one's husband has often meant maintaining the status quo, not doing anything too adventurous, and making sure the husband's wishes are put first in any decision. I have just finished reading the memoirs of an American woman who lived through the early days of the feminist movement. It rends my heart to read what was expected of her friends who married in the late 1950s, and the missed opportunities that so many of them weep for in their old age, when they look at today's Western women.

Today I believe that the Christian woman ought to be able to have her cake and eat it: pleasing the Lord should be the same as pleasing our husbands (not necessarily vice versa, as used to be the case). In any relationship, we ought to be able to release each other to be everything that God intends us to be.

....

Lord, help me to recognise when my worries about pleasing others are born of an unhealthy desire to avoid hurt or rejection. Give me the strength to be everything you intended me to be.

AHS

Angels with broken wings

'The younger son got together all he had, set off for a distant country and there squandered his wealth in wild living. After he had spent everything, there was a severe famine in that whole country, and he began to be in need.'

Not all women are mothers: there are many different reasons why that may be so, and reading about motherhood and children can be difficult for those who wish to be in that state but are not. Nevertheless, the fact cannot be avoided that one of the major sources of anxiety for women is their children. Even many childless women worry about caring for the children of dead relatives.

In the West, our concerns may not be as basic as those of our sisters in famine-ridden or war-torn countries, who worry on a daily basis about finding enough food or clean water for the children in their care. However, the current economic climate has made many of our lives very challenging: I have an acquaintance who practically starves herself every day and works extremely long hours so that her fatherless children can eat.

Many of the 'more fortunate' of us are concerned about children who have disappointed our expectations, children whom we have brought up 'in the way that they should go' (Proverbs 22:6) as well as we could manage and yet, in contrast to the apparent promise of scripture, have radically departed from that way. In such situations, we can only empathise with the unmentioned mother of the prodigal son, who I am sure would have watched and prayed just as hard as the father who stood constantly on lookout at the gate (v. 20). I can offer some solace from my own experience: 25 years of prayer and a child of her own eventually brought my sister-in-law to Christ. Persistence in prayer and unconditional love are the only answer.

....

Lord, help me never to give up on angels with broken wings. May I be there to bind up the broken-hearted and comfort those who mourn—be they parent or child.

AHS

The prayer of faith

Is any one of you in trouble? You should pray. Is anyone happy? Sing songs of praise

Over the last eight days I have taken time to look at aspects of fear—areas of our lives that cause us to worry and be anxious. Yesterday I touched on the only real answer to all these fear factors—prayer. Often, we remember that the answer to our problems is prayer only when those problems revolve around someone we love—usually a child or other relative. When the focus of our worries is on ourselves, we are more inclined to keep them to ourselves. Well, I know I do. For many women, the combination of our natural tendency to focus on the needs of others and the social reinforcement of that role by centuries of expectation from others (including women), means that we can keep our worries to ourselves rather than 'bother' God with them.

In today's reading from James 5, we read that if we are in trouble then we should pray. Although James doesn't follow this instruction with a clear statement that prayer will release us from our troubles, the inference from the rest of the passage is that prayer changes things—especially the prayer of the 'righteous person'. This reminds me of a sermon I recently heard from our pastor's wife in which she described how it was only when she got right with the Lord that the problem she was praying about found a solution. Sometimes we get in the way of the answer to our prayers because, in our pride, we are so sure we know the solution, and that solution is all we are praying for. Only when we are willing to accept that God might see things differently do we find that there is a 'ram in the thicket' (Genesis 22:13).

....

Father, in my focus on caring for others, I often forget that you care about me. Help me to bring my personal worries and concerns to you because I know you are waiting for me to do so.

AHS

Life laundry

Cast all your anxiety on him because he cares for you. Be self-controlled and alert. Your enemy the devil prowls around like a roaring lion looking for someone to devour.

When we moved house, I had to sort through twelve years of accumulated junk and reduce our possessions by at least 50 per cent. When you move out of a large vicarage into a small town house, downsizing is essential. Working through each room of the house in turn was not too difficult, but the task I dreaded most was clearing the attic. This was the place where we'd thrown all the old things that we hadn't been able to get rid of over the years. The contents of the attic weighed as heavily on my mind as they did on the rafters. Eventually I divided the space into sections and tackled each one in turn.

Deciding what to do with your stuff is not always easy. Some objects are associated with painful memories; some might have been expensive mistakes; some are heirlooms that you can't ditch even though you want to. Ultimately it is all a worry and a burden. I culled most of the rubbish but, when I look into the attic of our new home, there still seems to be a lot of stuff up there, even if it is neatly packed in labelled archive boxes.

Our lives have often been compared to houses. Clearing out the kitchen or the sitting-room of our lives can be hard work but it's relatively easy compared to facing the compounded emotional and spiritual junk we have chucked in the attic. My challenge to you today is to face up to the junk in the attic of your life—even if you have to deal with it bit by bit over the course of a year—and cast it all on the Lord to deal with. Then the worries and anxieties associated with it won't be able to consume you and you will be free to be all that the Lord intended you to be.

. . . .

Lord, help me to throw off everything that hinders and the sin that so easily entangles and run with perseverance the race marked out for me (see Hebrews 12:1).

AHS

A burden shared

I rejoice greatly in the Lord that at last you have renewed your concern for me… It was good of you to share in my troubles.

One way in which women differ from men is that we are more relational: we like to have a good gossip and talk about what is going on in our lives. Working in an office with six other women, I find that there is ample opportunity for sharing our personal concerns. Some of us have formidable worries and anxieties. Due to our average age, these worries centre mainly on the antics of older children and the ailments of ageing parents, but I have noticed, during two years in three similar offices, that being able to share her troubles is a great help to the woman going through the pain. It makes all the difference to know that someone has remembered to ask you how your sick mother fared over the weekend, or if things are any better for the daughter facing redundancy. It's a secular workplace so we don't go as far as to pray for each other openly, but I am sure there are several who use their ears and pray for their colleagues at home.

The troubles Paul is talking about in today's passage were rather different from the modern woman's day-to-day anxieties. One thing we can take home from what he has written, though, is the knowledge that a group of people has bothered to show practical concern for him has enabled him to rejoice in the Lord. Being able to rejoice in the face of our troubles breaks the power that the source of the worry has over us, and allows us to see it in perspective—ideally in the Lord's perspective. If the ability to share as a group of women in a secular environment has power to change a life, think how much more can be achieved if we commit to sharing and praying with women who believe.

Lord, forgive me for neglecting my friendships and being so self-centred. Help me to commit to renewing my concern for others, so that in turn I might have concern renewed for me.

AHS

Naked detachment

Who shall separate us from the love of Christ? Shall trouble or hardship or persecution or famine or nakedness or danger or sword? … [Nothing] in all creation will be able to separate us from the love of God that is in Christ Jesus our Lord.

During the process of moving house, I faced up to the fact that I am a control freak: hyper-organised but very fearful if I'm unable to predict or control what is going on around me in my private life or the future. I decided to deal with this item of emotional/spiritual junk in my life's attic and looked for a book that might help. I found a title that sounded as if it was a response to exactly what I was experiencing—*Embracing Uncertainty: achieving peace of mind as we face the unknown* by Susan Jeffers—so I bought it. The book turned out to be based mainly on Hindu and New Age spirituality that I had to approach with what my husband would call a 'resistant reading'—that is, a large pinch of salt. However, one thing it said was quite helpful—that if we surrender to the fact that we are unable to control the uncertainty, then we can 'breathe a huge sigh of relief' (p. 8). In other words, learning to accept that we can't control what is going to happen brings a sense of release.

In a way, I think this is what Paul is saying in today's reading. We don't know what we are going to have to face as ordinary human beings or because we are Christian believers. It might be hardship, poverty, physical assault, unacceptable pain and loss, spiritual opposition, difficulties in the present or the future (v. 38). In all this, though, one thing is certain: nothing can separate us from the love of God that is in Christ Jesus our Lord. Once we realise that his love is all that matters, we can trust God to take care of everything else with a strange sense of detachment.

....

Thank you, Lord, that whatever is going on around us your love is the constant point of stability in our lives. May we never lose sight of that focus.

AHS

Get up and do something about it

She… shut the door behind her and her sons. They brought the jars to her and she kept pouring. When all the jars were full, she said to her son, 'Bring me another one.' But he replied, 'There is not a jar left.' Then the oil stopped flowing.

I have heard many sermons preached on the story of Elisha and the widow's oil; most of them have focused on the miraculous multiplication of the oil into all the jars and vessels that the widow's sons could bring her, and the fact that the oil stopped flowing only when there were no more containers to hold it. This is a wonderful picture of God's provision—both physical and spiritual (oil symbolises the Holy Spirit)—but I want to look more closely at the woman herself. Obviously she was frantic with worry about what would happen to her and her sons now that her husband was dead. Elisha cut through her self-absorption and asked her, 'What do you have in your house?' It didn't take her long to take stock and say, 'Nothing… except a little oil.' Elisha gave her instructions to collect jars from her neighbours and pour out the oil, which then multiplied until the vessels were full.

I was once worrying about what might happen to me and my children if my husband died—as in that situation clergy wives lose their homes. Someone pulled me up short and said, 'You always make the most of what you have got.' This made me stop and take stock of what I did have, and I realised that I wasn't making the most of it but was letting it drift. As a result of that timely comment, I started my own business—small to start with, but it became a company that I ran for ten years. The income began to dry up only once I stopped 'bringing the vessels' and life took a new turn.

I want to encourage you not to wallow in self-pity over your worries, but to use them to spur you into action. Then you can watch as the Lord multiples your efforts.

....

Lord, help me to identify the 'oil' and the 'vessels' in my life that may be the hidden answer to my problems, and give me the inspiration and initiative to do something with them.

AHS

Comfort to spare

Praise be to the God and Father of our Lord Jesus Christ, the Father of compassion and the God of all comfort, who comforts us in all our troubles, so that we can comfort those in any trouble with the comfort we ourselves have received from God.

On Tuesday we looked at how helpful it is when we are able to share our burdens and worries with each other. Today I want to focus more specifically on how we, as believers, can be there to support others without expecting to get anything in return.

As time passes, the things that have caused us worry and anxiety recede into the past and we begin to see the fruit of that experience in our lives. If we have allowed the Lord to help us through a worrying time, the difficult experience will have left us a better person rather than a bitter person. It will have contributed to the maturing of deep spiritual character in us (2 Peter 1:3–9) and laid down another layer of wisdom in our lives.

We all ask from time to time why God allows people to suffer and go through great troubles. Ultimately, I don't know the answer to that but I do know that if we have come out of difficulties as a better person, we are equipped to help others who are going through the same kinds of problems. They can then become better people, too. Anne Frank, the Dutch Jewish diarist, wrote that 'our [women's] stories are all different, but all the same'. If you think about it, you will see that it is true. It doesn't matter if the 'BA' after a woman's name stands for Born Again or Bachelor of Arts—when push comes to shove, our lives can all be distilled down to the same spectrum of trials and temptations (1 Corinthians 10:13). I think our job, perhaps as older women, is to be there to listen to others and offer them the fruit of our experience if it seems appropriate to do so.

....

Lord, may the life experiences through which you've allowed me to pass put me into a position to speak with wisdom and have 'faithful instruction on my tongue' (see Proverbs 31:26).

AHS

Believe in the promise

'Do not be terrified; do not be discouraged, for the Lord your God will be with you wherever you go.'

When I began this set of meditations on worry and anxiety, I was quite anxious and worried myself. As I come to the end of them, I find that my sense of spiritual equilibrium has been restored as I have reminded myself of God's past faithfulness in all the aspects of life that I was allowing myself to fret about. In fact, there are many verses in the Bible that encourage us not to worry, fear or be anxious. I heard once that there are 365 verses in the Bible including the words 'Fear not'—one for each day of the year, so we need never be lacking encouragement that God is faithful and that he is with us. I suppose that statistic would depend on which version of the Bible was used and which keywords were typed into the search engine. However picky we want to be, though, we can't deny that the Bible is full of encouragements not to fear and promises that the Lord is faithful to those who trust in him. Here are a few of my favourites.

- The Lord is good, a refuge in times of trouble. He cares for those who trust in him (Nahum 1:7).
- 'So do not fear, for I am with you; do not be dismayed, for I am your God. I will strengthen you and help you; I will uphold you with my righteous right hand' (Isaiah 41:10).
- 'Do not let your hearts be troubled. Trust in God; trust also in me' (John 14:1).
- There is no fear in love. But perfect love drives out fear, because fear has to do with punishment. The one who fears is not made perfect in love (1 John 4:18).

....

Thank you, Lord, that your faithfulness towards me never fails and that you are with me wherever I go. Make me 'perfect in your love' so that I may have no need to fear.

AHS

What do you worry about? Since the start of the month, Alie Stibbe has been describing how she worried about the impact of a major upheaval in her family life: changing direction from life in parish ministry, moving house, changing jobs and all that it entailed. Whether or not you are facing a major upheaval in life, the solution to life's worries is the same for each of us: 'Cast all your anxiety on him because he cares for you' (1 Peter 5:7, NIV).

Talk to God about anything that worries you. Give problems to him and leave them with him. Easier said than done? Matthew, the Gospel writer, offers the solution: 'Seek first his kingdom and his righteousness, and all these things will be given to you as well. Therefore do not worry' (Matthew 6:33–34).

The solution to worry and anxiety is to change your focus. Focus on God, his goodness, his promises, his plans for our world; take courage as you focus on God's ability—not your disability or problems.

Over the next two weeks, Tracy Williamson will be helping us to refocus, to appreciate how much we are loved by God. Tracy is profoundly deaf, and she works alongside Marilyn Baker, who is blind. Their ministry, together and as individuals, has helped and encouraged thousands of people. It is a practical demonstration of what God can do when his people focus on God's ability rather than their own limitations, difficult background or challenging circumstances.

Over the next fortnight, keep your focus on God and his love for you and for those you meet. When worries come, hand them to God and reset your focus on him. Determine not to be distracted from focusing on our loving God. The problems of life loom large when they take all our attention, but, seen in the light of God's love and power, they take on different proportions.

Created in love

For you created my inmost being; you knit me together in my mother's womb. I praise you because I am fearfully and wonderfully made; your works are wonderful, I know that full well.

I read the above verses just after getting up and seeing myself in the mirror. I'd thought, 'What an old hag you're becoming!' but as I read this psalm I knew that God was speaking to me about my negative self-perception. He wanted me to rejoice in, not to despise, what he had made and to see myself as his wonderful work of creation.

I thought of the psalm's author, David. The words create a picture of him as a toddler in his heavenly Father's arms, relishing the sense that he is wholly cherished and loved. The words came to me: 'You are also wholly cherished and loved. Live in the truth of that.' I felt stunned, knowing that in many ways I hardly believe, let alone live by that assurance. Yet the whole of Psalm 139 expresses the joy that God feels in watching over us, his beloved creation. Wherever we are, whatever we are doing, whether we are 'up' or 'down', he knows and is with us. Sometimes we focus so much on the knowledge that 'I am a sinner saved by grace', we forget that the wonder of our creation is deeper than our sinfulness. we were made as the height of God's creation. Verses 13–14, printed above, shout out the fact that God poured love and care into every tiny detail of our body and being, writing uniqueness into our very DNA, our innermost self.

I have a friend who loves to paint. She delights in experimenting with ideas, colours and shapes. Soon a beautiful, unique picture begins to unfold on the blank canvas. This is God's heart as he works upon us, with joy and anticipation for what will be, breathing his very own life and genes into us. What a difference it would make if we really believed this and lived by the truth of it.

....

Read the above verses slowly, adding your own name: 'For you created [Tracy's] inmost being…' Tell Jesus you are sorry for any lies you've believed about yourself and ask him to write the truth on to your heart that you are cherished and loved and always have been.

TW

Slaves or children?

For those who are led by the Spirit of God are the children of God. The Spirit you received does not make you slaves, so that you live in fear again; rather, the Spirit you received brought about your adoption to sonship. And by him we cry, 'Abba, Father.'

Slavery is a concept that we don't often encounter in the West and we can have a particular mindset about it. Maybe we envisage a starved, ragged figure, chained to a master, obeying his every command. Although that picture may be in line with what Paul knew of slavery, he was actually referring to the difference between feeling inwardly controlled, thus motivated by fear, and delighting in the knowledge that we are chosen and belong to God as his beloved children.

It doesn't take much to think of things that enslave us: the need to conform or to achieve, to acquire success; money or possessions; addictions; anger, fear or bitterness through experiencing others' demands, judgments and rejections. The list could go on for ever. You know what inwardly controls you or makes you fearful, but God gives you something very different. His own Spirit comes to you as a friend, to lead you and give life to you. He speaks wonderful insights into your heart about your true identity. He frees you to be yourself.

'Leading' in this context is a gentle word. My friend Marilyn is blind so I lead her by the hand. I don't force her to go where I want to go. I find out where she wants to go and then help her get there. I respect her as we plan what we are going to do, and our contact is one of trust and love. Conversely, I am deaf so Marilyn tells me what others are saying and so encourages me. She is not interfering but simply rejoicing in helping me to be a valued member of a group.

Can these parallels become a picture to you? Will you let the Holy Spirit show you that God loves and trusts you and makes you his child and heir?

....

*'But whenever anyone turns to the Lord, the veil is taken away.
Now the Lord is the Spirit, and where the Spirit of the Lord is,
there is freedom' (2 Corinthians 3:16, NIV).*

TW

Beloved sons and daughters

While he was still a long way off, his father saw him coming. Filled with love and compassion, he ran to his son, embraced him, and kissed him.

This is a beautiful story, but do we really apply its truths to ourselves? Jesus wanted to point people to the heart of the Father, to show that God is loving and compassionate, delighting in his children, believing in them even while feeling their pain, celebrating over them when they turn to him.

Most of us don't mess up in such a dramatic way as the younger son in the parable, but Jesus wanted to show that whatever mistakes we make, God never stops loving us and always wants to restore us as his beloved children.

Soon after I became a Christian, someone's chance remark ignited my years of buried hurt and I ran away in an explosion of boiling emotions. I was at college at the time but I swore that I was never going back and that I had been deceived in believing in God. Hours later, I stumbled into a bus shelter on a dark country road. It was stormy, so even the weather fitted my mood. I cannot hear speech but suddenly I heard a voice speak so clearly that I leapt up: 'I love you and want to be a father to you.' I looked around but of course there was no one there. It was God. He was with me, loving me despite my anger. He then spoke into my heart of the kind of Father he wanted to be to me: to share my struggles and joys, to speak words of love and help to me, to listen to me, to heal, comfort and guide me. He longed for me to know and go to him as a child runs trustingly to her daddy.

That experience was the beginning of my living as God's beloved daughter. He longs for you to live that adventure, too. Have you begun?

....

'All I want to do is to bless you. All I want to do is pour out my love. To show you how dear you are to me, for me there is no other. To me you are the pearl of great price.'
THE FATHER'S SONG OF LOVE © MARILYN BAKER

TW

Release from shame 1

As she stood behind him at his feet weeping, she began to wet his feet with her tears. Then she wiped them with her hair, kissed them and poured perfume on them.

A beautiful fruit of living as God's beloved is freedom from the crippling manifestations of shame. Shame is like a beast strangling us with its tentacles of lies and accusations. It comes through our own unresolved guilt and the effects of others' treatment of us. It is the heart conviction that 'I am bad' and it holds us in a vice of regret and worthlessness. For years I couldn't hug or even make eye contact with anyone because of the shame of being abused. I could hardly speak because of the effects of verbal mockery. Natural weaknesses like my deafness became huge flaws that paralysed me. I constantly struggled with thoughts like, 'They'll only have to look at you to see what a failure you are.'

As this woman in Luke 7 discovered, however, Jesus loves us completely and he gently lifts off every weight of shame. Maybe she had already seen how Jesus loved people who were hurt. All we know is that when she gatecrashed the party, her prison of shame had already cracked. All she wanted was to love and thank Jesus. She expressed it in the only way she could—with overflowing, uninhibited tears and actions. Others tried to heap yet more judgment upon her but Jesus' response heals us all: he affirmed her actions as being a source of deep blessing to him, ending with the words 'Your faith has saved you; go in peace' (v. 50).

Jesus gladly gives you this same peace. One day, looking at a cross, I prayed, 'Jesus help me.' Suddenly he spoke: 'I did this for you. I love you. Live in my love.' An incredible shaft of love poured into my heart. I felt overwhelmed. All I could do was weep—healing tears. Yes, I am weak, but now all my crippling shame has gone.

....

Thank you, Lord Jesus, that you died so I could be free from shame. Pour your healing love and truth into every imprisoned area of my life. Set me free to live and love without fear. Amen

TW

Release from shame 2

Therefore, there is now no condemnation for those who are in Christ Jesus… Those he predestined, he also called; those he called, he also justified; those he justified, he also glorified.

As we saw yesterday, Jesus said to the woman who anointed him, 'Your faith has saved you; go in peace.' It's wonderful to have a deep experience of God but we need to learn to live in the truth of it. Even while the woman was pouring out her gratitude to Jesus, Simon the Pharisee was muttering negatives about her. What would happen when she went home, surrounded by people who had known her at her worst and judged her accordingly? Jesus wanted her to take hold of his peace and live in it, to silence the negatives by telling them (and therefore Satan), 'I am totally forgiven and loved by Jesus.'

The fact is, we will always need to choose whose words we accept as the truth. Paul expresses the heart of Jesus in Romans 8: 'There is now no condemnation.' We are 'called', 'justified', 'glorified'. God does not just release us into limbo, but sets us free to step fully into the calling he has for us, to reveal his glory in the unique way that only you or I can.

I mentioned yesterday that once I could hardly speak because of past mockery. Jesus began a deep work in me. He spoke to me as I read the Bible and prayed. I had to renounce lies that I had believed about myself. I begged him to release me to express my personality in such a way that others would see him. He gave me a verse to act as an antidote to the lies: Isaiah 50:4. It says, 'The Sovereign Lord has given me an instructed tongue, to know the word that sustains the weary.' He was nudging me to start to speak out, to expect him to give me words to help others. It was, and still can be, hard to break through my fears, but now I am testifying, teaching, prophesying and praying for people who are hurt.

···

*'We know that in all things God works for the good of those who love him, who have been called according to his purpose'
(Romans 8:28).*

TW

Laying down cultural pressures

[Jesus] came to a village where a woman named Martha opened her home to him. She had a sister called Mary, who sat at the Lord's feet listening to what he said. But Martha was distracted by all the preparations that had to be made.

Like many women, I find myself pulled in different directions by diverse responsibilities. I look around and think, 'I must get that done now!' Then I scurry here and there trying to do everything. Someone will say, 'You need to prioritise.' I agree and love the idea—yet how do you prioritise when everything is urgent?

This story about Mary and Martha always speaks to me. Both women loved Jesus and wanted to give him the very best, but whereas, for Mary, that desire sprang out of her heart knowledge that she was loved, Martha was motivated by fear—the fear of not living up to the cultural expectations of others.

How was Mary able to make the choice to sit at Jesus' feet and ignore the pull within her to be what everyone expected her to be? She must have been very aware of her sister's obvious resentment as she bustled about. The difference for Mary was that she believed, deep inside herself, that she was loved by Jesus. Such a belief changes us. It is as if a well of peace is created in our hearts. Out of that well, Mary was able to discern that the most vital requirement in that moment was to concentrate on loving Jesus, by simply listening to him, honouring him and cherishing his words.

Maybe, as Jesus arrived and Mary looked up and saw him, a God-given awareness came that he would not be around for much longer. Such insight into the ways of God comes only to those who live as his beloved in their everyday choices, rather than just by contemporary customs. Jesus said to Martha, 'Only one thing is needed. Mary has chosen what is better, and it will not be taken away from her' (v. 42).

....

John said, 'We love because he first loved us' (1 John 4:19). Jesus, please help me, like Mary, to make choices that are 'better', that spring out of the knowledge that I am loved and free me to love truly in response.

TW

The power of thankfulness

Sacrifice thank-offerings to God, fulfil your vows to the Most High, and call upon me in the day of trouble; I will deliver you, and you will honour me.

Recently I have struggled to start the day positively. It seems that as soon as I wake up I become aware of all the things that have the potential to go wrong, and I often feel like diving straight back under the covers. The phrase 'sacrifice thank-offerings' in this passage caught my attention. Here's a reality check: God asks us to choose to be thankful. Thankfulness is not about having gooey feelings: if that were the case, it might never happen for some of us. Sacrifice is all about choice and cost, but as we make that choice it's as if a door is opened in our circumstances. We see God working on our behalf and we are changed deep inside.

A disabled friend was challenged by a sermon on thankfulness. The next day she had to see the doctor to have her incapacity benefit confirmed—always a humiliating procedure. She remembered the sermon and started thanking God that he is loving and faithful in all his ways. The doctor's surgery was busy and she had to wait a long time to be seen. When she was eventually called, she was so stiff from sitting that she could barely walk. The doctor, who had previously dismissed her condition, took one look at her, said, 'Of course you need the benefit' and immediately signed the form. My friend then wasn't sure how she would walk home but two young girls came and supported her on either side, walking with her right to her flat. She was amazed and was convinced they were angels.

My friend's natural feeling had been to dread the appointment and believe the worst but she chose to be thankful despite those feelings. After seeing what God had done, thankfulness and joy were welling up naturally from the deepest part of her being.

....

Make the choice today to bring God a sacrifice of thanksgiving, whatever your feelings or your circumstances. Thank him for who he is and for all he does. Then see how he works on your behalf.

TW

Hearing we are loved

'If you remain in me and my words remain in you, ask whatever you wish, and it will be given you. This is to my Father's glory, that you bear much fruit, showing yourselves to be my disciples. As the Father has loved me, so have I loved you.'

This is one of those passages that is so familiar, we can rush through it thinking, 'I know this!' I find it one of the most dynamic passages in the Bible, though, one that reveals Jesus' key to powerful, effective ministry and releases us into the same ministry. Here is the foundation stone of our status as God's beloved—Jesus words, 'As the father has loved me, so have I loved you' (v. 9). He goes on to say, 'Now remain in my love.'

Have you really taken time to drink this in? This is what 'remain in my love' means—thinking about it, basking and revelling in it, speaking it out as a healing truth into inner areas of hurt or unbelief. We should be shouting 'Wow!' and dancing around. Think how much God the Father loves the Son: now Jesus says that you are loved in exactly the same way. It is a life-changing truth, vital for us to hear.

A disabled woman at a conference was praying. She felt low about herself. She said to the Lord, 'There are so many things I can't do'—and he said, 'I love you.' She said, 'But I can't walk and I'm so awkward socially'—and he said, 'I love you.' She had never been able to hear him and that was yet another factor in her self-despising. Now she realised that she could hear him; she just hadn't listened with expectancy before. He simply told her over and over again, 'I love you', but deep within her heart she heard him and something changed. On the last day of the conference she shared how she had started worshipping expressively, using her body in a way she had never felt free to do before. What a beautiful, wonderful witness to the power of hearing God's love.

....

Jesus says to you, 'I love you.' Have you heard him today? Will you believe his words of love and bask in the joy of them?

TW

Listening in everyday life 1

'Suppose a woman has ten silver coins and loses one. Does she not light a lamp, sweep the house and search carefully until she finds it? And when she finds it, she calls her friends and neighbours together and says, "Rejoice with me; I have found my lost coin."'

One of the joys of knowing we are God's beloved is the realisation that every part of our everyday life matters to him and can be a channel for his voice. Think of Jesus' illustrations demonstrating God's heart of love for those lost in sin. It's a powerful, important message but he spoke it through the medium of understandable everyday scenarios. Here we see a woman who has lost something precious. Jesus could well have been relating a situation that he had witnessed. Look at the detail in his story: the tender way he describes her efforts to find the coin—lighting the lamp, sweeping the floor—her intense concentration, her inability to focus on anything except what is missing, and then her joy and celebration on its discovery. The wonderful thing is that Jesus experienced the heart of his Father God through this woman. She has been a picture to him, and now he uses that same picture to reveal God's heart to others.

Do you realise that the way you live your life can reflect God to others? Believe that Jesus is with you in whatever you do today. He is watching over you, lovingly taking everything in. He wants to be involved and to speak to you in the different situations you face. Once, like the woman in the parable, I lost something very important—my glasses, without which I can't see. I hunted everywhere, to no avail. As I prayed, I sensed Jesus say, 'Look in the van.' That seemed ridiculous as we hadn't travelled in the van for several days. Eventually, though, I did look and found my glasses among the PA equipment in the back. I had taken them off when sorting something out earlier. I had forgotten but my friend Jesus knew and cared.

....

It's amazing, Jesus, how lovingly you watch over me. Let me hear your voice in my everyday situations. Help me to live in such a way that I can be a true reflection of God's heart to others around me. Amen

TW

Listening in everyday life 2

'Do not worry about your life, what you will eat or drink; or about your body, what you will wear… Look at the birds of the air; they do not sow or reap or store away in barns, and yet your heavenly Father feeds them. Are you not much more valuable than they?'

I love this passage. We women often worry secretly. We manage our lives but deep down we struggle with all sorts of anxieties—not least about how we will provide for our families or what we will wear. Here Jesus shows us how deeply God cares about the tiniest details of our lives. I find it really exciting to think that I might hear him in my everyday routine and jobs. It was like a light turning on inside me when I realised that Jesus tuned in to his Father and received deep insights and understanding through ordinary things, like a woman and her coin, farmers planting seeds, builders building and house-wives baking bread.

In this particular story Jesus tells us to 'look' at the birds—really look. The Greek word means to use all our senses, to study from all sides, think about and touch. Then we need to listen in our hearts to what God wants to say through them, as here: 'Are you not much more valuable than they?'

Hearing God like this can transform our daily lives and faith. Do you expect him to touch you in this way? It is like a secret language between friends. I was once eating chicken. I put the wishbone aside but kept seeing myself as a child, pulling the wishbone with my mum. If our thoughts zoom in on something like this, it can be a sign that God wants to speak, so I asked him rather sceptically. The thought immediately came back to me that I was praying in the way I pulled that wishbone—just as a ritual. He said, 'I'm not a wishbone, I'm your heavenly Father, and I want to answer your prayers.' I was dumbstruck. It was true, but I would never have known if he hadn't shown me.

....

When a newborn baby comes into the world; when you see a rose, its petals all unfurled, is it chance or science or the whispers of God?
WHISPERS OF GOD © MARILYN BAKER

TW

Stepping into your calling

The angel said to her, 'Do not be afraid, Mary, you have found favour with God. You will be with child and give birth to a son, and you are to give him the name Jesus. He will be great and will be called the Son of the Most High.'

What was it that caused Mary to find such favour with God? The Bible does not say, but we get a glimpse as we see her reaction to the angel's earth-shattering news. Yes, she is afraid. This is encouraging, for who doesn't feel thrown at the prospect of huge disruptions in life? Yet Mary does not allow those feelings to prevent her from hearing everything the angel has to tell her.

Sometimes my reactions so overwhelm me that I dismiss ideas without properly listening. Mary was very confused, but she communicated her confusion to the angel: 'How will this be… since I am a virgin?' (v. 34). Asking questions to help us grow in understanding is very important. I call it 'healing dialogue' and use a laptop or journal to raise my confusions with God and listen for his answers. God loves to engage with us and counsel us when he sees that our heart attitude is one of faith and receptivity. Think of Mary's response at the end: 'I am the Lord's servant… May it be to me as you have said' (v. 38).

Those words reveal why Mary found favour with God. She was willing to step trustingly into her calling, whatever the cost. God never promises us an easy ride. Being beloved never means that our circumstances will always be cushy and safe. Rather, it means that God calls us to partner with him in bringing to birth his greatest plans and purposes. Mary was young, poor and humanly inadequate to fulfil this call. Moreover, she faced misunderstanding, probable divorce, even death, if she agreed. Yet being a trusted part of all that God was doing was more important to her than being safe and respectable.

I would love that to be my heart's response, too. What about you?

....

Thank you, Lord, for Mary's heart of trust. Thank you that while she was so real in her responses she still listened to you. Work in my heart, dear Lord, so that I can find such favour with you and help to bring your purposes to birth today. Amen

TW

You are here for a purpose

Mordecai… sent back this answer: 'Do not think that because you are in the king's house you alone of all the Jews will escape… Who knows but that you have come to royal position for such a time as this?'

Esther's story is challenging. Life can seem very humdrum. That's as true for me as anyone else, even though I am in an 'exciting' itinerant ministry. The grassroots of that ministry is washing or packing—with the intermittent high of seeing someone meet with the Lord in a wonderful way. For most of us, mundane tasks far outweigh anything else. Maybe, like me, you sometimes think, 'Is it all worth it?'

Esther also experienced the dullness of routine. After all the months of anticipation, beauty treatments, the heady exhilaration of being chosen as queen and the fanfare of celebrations, now came the humdrum living out of her life between each royal summons: 'Thirty days have passed since I was called to go to the king' (v. 11).

However, there is always a bigger picture that God alone can see and for which, incredibly, he has set us in place. Life is fragile. Perhaps our whole nation is not under threat of annihilation, as Esther's was, but we hear daily news of stabbings, child abuse, political corruption, terrorist attacks, disease pandemics and recession. We can react by hiding our faces (as was Esther's first response) or we can hear in our own hearts, 'Who knows but that you have come to royal position for such a time as this?' (v. 14).

Mordecai's prophetic words changed Esther into a woman of tremendous courage. She stopped saying 'I can't' and started praying, 'Lord, what can I do?' Through prayer she received the strength to identify with her people, whatever the cost. God didn't turn her into a great stateswoman; instead he used her womanly gifts of beauty, homemaking and understanding to defeat the enemy's strategy totally. It was a role that only she could fulfil. How does God want to use you?

....

'God wants just you, yes, no one else will do. Listen to him call you by name. You were in his plan before the world began, and he longs that you live your life for him.'
'GOD HAS A PLAN FOR YOU' © MARILYN BAKER

TW

Loving as he loves us

Love is patient, love is kind. It does not envy, it does not boast, it is not proud. It is not rude, it is not self-seeking, it is not easily angered, it keeps no record of wrongs… It always protects, always trusts, always hopes, always perseveres. Love never fails.

I have been hurt in life, and it is an ongoing source of healing to know that in God's eyes I am beloved. He sees the beauty of his Son in me. He delights in speaking affirming words and using me to fulfil his purposes. It is incredible! Yet when I come to this passage, I stop in my tracks. This is the true test: am I really living my life as God's beloved? Do I love others as he loves me? Do I see them as equally beloved—even when they hurt me?

If I write my own name, 'Tracy', in place of 'love', I only have to read a short way before I am forced to answer 'no'. I can be patient, but often I am not. I can be kind, and long to be, but I frequently find myself thinking unkind thoughts. Sadly, I often do find that I've kept a record of wrongs, which surges out at the first opportunity. Is there any hope for me, for any of us? Can we really love in this radical way? If it is possible, we truly hold the key to changing the world.

There is an answer, and it lies in that last phrase: 'Love never fails.' When Paul wrote these amazing words through the Holy Spirit, it was significant that he addressed them to 'love' rather than to us. We are weak but God's love never fails. It is he who is kind, who keeps no record of wrongs.

How deeply will I open myself to his love? Will I let him comfort me? Will I believe that he trusts me? Will I accept that I am forgiven? Like thirsty plants, the beautiful blooms of love will flower as I drink in his love, which saturates my very roots.

....

Pour your life-giving waters into my depths, Lord Jesus. Your love alone never fails. Quench my thirst and fill me so that I can love as you love. Amen

TW

Empowered in love

Then Peter said, 'Silver and gold I do not have, but what I have I give you. In the name of Jesus Christ of Nazareth, walk.' Taking him by the right hand, he helped him up, and instantly the man's feet and ankles became strong. He jumped to his feet and began to walk.

This is a dynamic story—a miracle of heart-transformation. Peter now knows that he has an incredible treasure within him, giving him a security previously unknown, despite all his fire and passion. What is that treasure? It's the knowledge that he is loved by Jesus with a love that is true and real, embracing him despite his weaknesses.

Even though Peter had failed, Jesus' call on his life remains. It's as if he has taken one step into a slightly different place in a beautiful garden. It has the same view but now he is in the sunshine, not the shade, and everything looks and feels different. Instead of reactions of impetuosity, we see the maturity of Peter's new standpoint as the situation unfolds. He neither rushes in nor turns away when the man first accosts him. Instead, 'Peter looked straight at him' and then asked the man to 'look at us' (v. 4). In that short pause, Peter made an inner choice to listen, above everything else, for the heart of Jesus. Out of that choice came the certainty of conviction—'Silver and gold I do not have, but what I have I give you'—and the resulting miracle.

Do you know the treasure you have in Jesus? Have you allowed him to fill that fearful place deep within you? Peter acknowledged what he didn't have but then moved on and took hold of his true resources.

I am always so aware of my weaknesses. I can make a mountain out of my deafness or my childhood struggles, but Jesus calls me to listen for his word. As I do so, he does wonderful things, touching people's lives with healing power.

You and I are weak but he calls us 'Beloved' and gives us the treasure of his presence. Let's live in the sunshine of his empowering.

....

Lord Jesus, thank you that you have called me to do the works of your kingdom. Help me, like Peter, to live from a different centre— not out of what I don't have but out of the joy of who you are and what you have put within me. Amen

TW

What are you focusing on? Over the past fortnight, Tracy Williamson has helped us to focus on God's love for us. Knowing that we are loved can transform even the darkest situations.

I've come across many people whose lives have been deeply affected by traumatic circumstances: family breakdown, abuse or injustice. Some have never recovered. Deep emotional or mental wounds have left them unable to cope. Others, who have faced similarly debilitating situations, have gone on to recover, leaving the experiences behind.

What makes the difference? In many of the situations I've come across, love has transformed damaged lives. People who have come to know that they are unconditionally loved, wanted and appreciated can rise above many of the traumas of life. Love heals deep wounds and allows hurting people to find wholeness.

Over the next two weeks, Margaret Killingray will be taking us through the second half of her studies in Matthew's Gospel. As you meet Jesus again in these Gospel chapters, ask God for fresh insight and apprciation of his love, especially if you have known the stories of Jesus for many years. Try using an unfamiliar Bible translation to see Jesus from different perspectives as you seek to know him better.

Make this your prayer:

Thanks be to thee, my Lord Jesus Christ,
for all the benefits thou hast given me,
for all the pains and insults thou hast borne for me.
O most merciful redeemer, friend and brother,
may I know thee more clearly,
love thee more dearly,
and follow thee more nearly, day by day.
Amen

ST RICHARD OF CHICHESTER

Judging by appearances

'Isaiah was right… "These people honour me with their lips, but their hearts are far from me. They worship me in vain; their teachings are merely human rules." … Listen and understand. What goes into your mouth does not defile you, but what comes out of your mouth, that is what defiles you.'

For the next fortnight we will be reading the second half of Matthew's Gospel. You may remember how Jesus had been challenged by the Jewish teachers of the law. They had strong ideas about the right way to please God, so when they saw Jesus' disciples failing to wash their hands before eating, they accused them of breaking the religious rules.

Christians are sometimes tempted to make the same kinds of accusations—criticising what people wear to church and what they do on Sunday; telling a 14-year-old that her top is too low-cut when she's new to the youth group; telling an old man that he shouldn't buy lottery tickets before he's understood the gospel. We can judge by appearances, assuming that keeping the 'rules' is what matters, when we ourselves have made up the rules without finding out what God wants. Jesus called the teachers 'hypocrites' because they ruled that if someone pledged money to the temple, they could then avoid supporting their elderly parents, thus disobeying one of God's basic laws.

Jesus went on to point out that we can do all the 'right' things—whether it's washing our hands and avoiding certain foods, or singing loudly and saying 'amen'—but if our hearts are corrupt then we are unclean. We may turn up at all the church meetings, where we are seen, but avoid visiting people who are housebound or cooking for the harassed, where we are not seen.

This is also an Old Testament theme: 'I despise your religious festivals… Away with the noise of your songs! … But let justice roll on like a river, righteousness like a never-failing stream (Amos 5:21, 23–24).

....

When are you tempted to be critical? Is that criticism always fair?

MK

Peter: rock and stumbling block

'But what about you?' [Jesus] asked. 'Who do you say I am?' Simon Peter answered, 'You are the Messiah, the Son of the living God.' Jesus replied, 'Blessed are you, Simon son of Jonah… You are Peter, and on this rock I will build my church.'

Jesus asked his disciples the most important question, and Peter answered with a flash of revelation from God. Matthew was recording this conversation after the resurrection, when they all knew that Jesus was the Messiah for whom they had hoped and prayed for so long. Here, though, Peter had a glimpse of the amazing truth that this man—at the time, known simply as a man, his friend and teacher—was much more than they had hoped for. As a result, Jesus called him Peter, meaning 'rock', the rock on which the Church would be built.

The disciples and the crowds who followed Jesus still hoped that he would do what the Messiah should do—free Israel from pagan rule, cleanse the temple and restore David's kingdom in all its glory. So Jesus told his disciples not to tell the crowds that he was the Messiah, because it was not going be as they hoped. Instead he would be betrayed, arrested and killed. Peter took him on one side and told him off for being so 'silly': of course that wouldn't happen to him. 'Peter,' said Jesus, 'you are a stumbling block to me.'

It seems surprising that Peter would acknowledge the authority of Jesus and then tell him he couldn't mean what he said. Yet, as Christians, we are prone to do exactly that. We acknowledge him as God, Creator and Redeemer, our Lord and King, and then we act as if he cannot mean what he says. We know he forgives us but sometimes we find it hard to forgive others. He told us to love our neighbours as ourselves. He even told us to love our enemies, to do good to them and pray for them. Just like Peter, we sometimes think we know better.

....

Lord, help me to be like Peter in acknowledging you as my Saviour and Lord. Help me to obey you in everything I do.

MK

We beheld his glory

Jesus took with him Peter, James and John… and led them up a high mountain by themselves. There he was transfigured before them. His face shone like the sun… A bright cloud covered them, and a voice from the cloud said, 'This is my Son, whom I love; with him I am well pleased. Listen to him!'

This must have been an overwhelming moment for Peter, James and John. 'We were eyewitnesses of his majesty… We ourselves heard this voice that came from heaven when we were with him on the sacred mountain,' Peter wrote in his second letter (2 Peter 1:16, 18). Yet, coming down from the mountain, Jesus told them not to tell anyone about the vision until after he had risen from the dead. Why did he say that? Wouldn't it have served as proof that he was the Son of God? But not until after the crucifixion and resurrection would they realise that Jesus the man was both the glorified Lord of heaven, sitting at the right hand of God as Judge and Saviour, and the victim, bleeding and dying on a cross. It was almost impossible for them to understand that their teacher, the Lord's Messiah, would die as an executed criminal.

Yet there were hints in the Old Testament that should have given them a clue to the path he would take. 'He was despised and rejected by others, a man of suffering…. he was pierced for our transgressions' (Isaiah 53:3, 5). Tom Wright points out the strange parallels between the transfiguration and the crucifixion: here revealed in glory, there in shame; here in clothes shining white, there stripped of his clothes; here with Moses and Elijah, there with two thieves; here with a bright cloud round him, there in darkness (see *Matthew for Everyone*, SPCK, 2002).

Like the disciples, we should find this vision overwhelming—one that fills us with love and praise. Here is our Lord, a man, a human being like us, who knows the glory of heaven but walks to his death for love of you and me.

Sometimes it helps our understanding to read these stories and to recreate them in our imagination as onlookers and participants.

MK

Who is greatest?

He called a little child, whom he placed among them. And he said: 'Truly I tell you, unless you change and become like little children, you will never enter the kingdom of heaven. Therefore, whoever takes a humble place—becoming like this child—is the greatest in the kingdom of heaven.'

Christians are subjects of the king—they belong in the kingdom of God, under the rule of God—and in this chapter Matthew records Jesus' teaching about relationships in the kingdom. The disciples came to Jesus to ask who is the greatest in the kingdom of heaven. I wonder what was behind this question. As his chosen Twelve, did they dream of sitting at the top table when he was revealed as the Messiah?

'Who is the greatest?' is simply the wrong question, though. The issue does not arise under God's rule. Jesus teaches them the truth that all are of equal worth and all are called to humility, and he does this in several ways. We need to lack any awareness of status, like a child. Even the most insignificant person is to be welcomed as if they were Jesus himself. I remember hearing of a tramp who wandered into a large suburban church and sprawled in the empty front pew. One man immediately got up and walked forward. Most people were expecting him simply to help the man up and out, but he sat next to him, shared his Bible with him and welcomed him.

The shepherd (v. 12), Jesus said, rejoices more over the rescued lost sheep than the 99 who stayed smugly in the field. We rescue lost sheep because we know what it is to be rescued ourselves by the good shepherd. Humility is not about putting ourselves down and practising being a doormat. It is about rejoicing in being a rescued sheep and not noticing social status and importance for ourselves or anyone else.

....

Whether at work, at home or in church, can we identify when and why we are tempted to feel superior—and pray about it?

Read Philippians 2:5–8 to discover more about Jesus' attitude of mind.

MK

It's never going to be easy

Jesus replied, 'Moses permitted you to divorce your wives because your hearts were hard... Anyone who divorces his wife, except for sexual immorality, and marries another woman commits adultery.' The disciples said to him, 'If this is the situation between a husband and wife, it is better not to marry.'

If you are reading through each chapter each day, you will see that there is much more going on than these notes can cover. In this chapter, the disciples try to stop parents bringing children to Jesus; a rich young man loves his wealth too much to follow Jesus; and Jesus promises that all the losses, disappointments and sacrifices of following him will be put right in the glory of his eternal kingdom.

As the rich man turned away, Jesus remarked that it was hard for the rich to enter the kingdom of heaven (v. 23). Then the disciples began to see that it wouldn't be easy to live the kingdom life in this difficult world. Riches were one problem; divorce was another. The verses on divorce make difficult reading. How did the people of the time understand Moses' words (Deuteronomy 24:1–4) and what does the Greek word *porneia*, translated 'sexual immorality', really mean?

We can see two very important truths in Jesus' answers to the challenging question, 'Is it lawful for a man to divorce his wife for any and every reason?' First, he went back to Genesis 1:27 and pointed out that God's perfect will was that marriage should be a lifelong, exclusive relationship. He added that there would be those who did not marry, as he had not. Second, he pointed out that Moses had permitted divorce because of people's 'hardness of heart'. Sometimes marriages do break down. Then it might be better legally to end an already broken marriage and allow remarriage; but still, God's perfect way, the way that best serves the interests of adults and children, is marriage for life.

....

There are difficulties living in a society with a wide gulf between common practice and Christian ideals. There are books, DVDs and courses to aid group discussion.

MK

That's not fair!

'Friend, I am not being unfair to you. Didn't you agree to work for a denarius? Take your pay and go. I want to give the one who was hired last the same as I gave you… Are you envious because I am generous?'

Life is not always fair and we can become mean and grudging pretty easily. It's hard to be glad at someone else's good fortune, and equally hard, when the good fortune comes our way, to share generously. Listening to a friend just back from *another* holiday while we have to spend time with a frail mother-in-law; watching someone else's child get the prize when yours worked far harder—if we cultivate a resentful, unforgiving, mean nature, it will have plenty to work on. Life is unfair—terribly unfair for some—and there is always someone richer, cleverer, promoted sooner, prettier or slimmer than we are, for no good reason that we can see.

The landowner in this story pays all his workers one denarius—a fair day's wage—but he pays it to those who worked all day and to those who could only do an hour's work. 'It's not fair,' the first group said. 'We've borne the burden of the work and the heat of the day.' Yet give a thought to the ones who stood all day in the heat, getting more and more anxious about feeding their families when no one hired them, and rejoice at the caring generosity of the landowner.

'The Son of Man did not come to be served, but to serve, and to give his life as a ransom for many' (v. 28). This is God, the Creator, choosing to serve his creations; God, the Saviour, choosing to die for those who deliberately chose to reject him. So when Jesus tells the story of the generous landowner and his vineyard, he says that this is what the kingdom of heaven is like—the kingdom that we are working for here on earth. So as we accept the amazing generosity of a loving Saviour, we practise ungrudging generosity of spirit in our turn.

....

Read Leviticus 19:9–10 for another word about generosity. Where could we be generous in a similar way?

MK

He changed his mind

'There was a man who had two sons. He went to the first and said, "Son, go and work today in the vineyard." "I will not," he answered, but later he changed his mind and went. Then the father went to the other son and said the same thing. He answered, "I will, sir," but he did not go.'

There are two kinds of people—the ones who say 'yes' politely but walk away, and those who rudely say 'no', then feel bad, change their minds and do as they were asked.

Jesus rode triumphantly into Jerusalem like a king. The people rejoiced: the Messiah, the son of David, was coming to claim his city and its temple. But he rode in on a donkey, not a proud horse; then he knocked over the tables in the temple where the doves to be sacrificed were sold and set up his own ministry of healing. The chief priests and teachers challenged his authority. By what right could he stride into the temple, clear the money tables, and welcome the poor, the blind and the lame? 'Truly I tell you,' Jesus said to them, 'the tax collectors and the prostitutes are entering the kingdom of God ahead of you' (v. 31).

The key thing about tax collectors and prostitutes—outcasts, the ones with dodgy jobs, those who were despised—was that they knew they were out of favour; they knew that society saw them as people who had said 'no' to godly living. Because they knew this, they changed their minds. They heard Jesus' message, felt his healing hand and accepted God's mercy. The religious ones didn't think they needed mercy. They had said 'yes' but had then shut their hearts to God's claims.

Jesus told them that only the people whose 'yes' to God is 'yes' to a changed mind and heart, and to lifelong discipleship in obedience to his will, can be part of the kingdom. The priests and the Pharisees knew he was telling them that, unless they changed, they would be excluded, so they began to plot to arrest him.

....

When life is busy and full of people and demands, it is easy to say, 'Yes, I will' and then walk away. Give yourself time to remember the commitments you have made.

MK

A wedding banquet for a son

'Then he said to his servants, "The wedding banquet is ready, but those I invited did not deserve to come. Go to the street corners and invite to the banquet anyone you find." So the servants went out… and gathered all the people they could find, the bad as well as the good.'

The parable of the vineyard tenants at the end of chapter 21 is similar to this one about the wedding banquet. In his love, God gave the law and the prophets to show the people of Israel the right way to live. Finally, because they had failed to listen and had rejected his rule, he sent his Son to live and die, to bring Israelites, and all his world, back into a relationship with him.

Jesus was speaking to the religious leaders of the Jewish nation; they were the ones who had refused the invitation to the wedding. So the invitation goes to those shunned by polite religious society, 'the bad as well as the good'. It's a wonderful picture: there is the great hall with a feast laid out, and in come the people off the streets, the rough and the tough, the disabled and the beggars, the prostitutes and the thieves. God loves everyone. If people won't come when he invites them, they have made their choice and they will have to suffer the consequences.

Then there's a 'but…'. God does love everyone, sinners though we all are, but we cannot stay as we are. We have to change. When the sick and blind came to Jesus, he healed them; when the tax collectors came, they had to give back the money they had stolen. We must come in the garment of repentance: the man in the story who did not was thrown out (v. 13). Then, in verses 37–39, we are reminded that this loving God, who invites us into his kingdom and to his banquet, requires us to love in return—first to love him with all our heart, and second to love our neighbours, whoever they are. Then, in the end, we will sit down with him at the wedding feast of the Lamb.

••

Read Revelation 19:7–9 and rejoice that feasts and food are so important in the Bible. Hospitality is one way in which we can share the joy of the kingdom of God.

MK

Woe betide you!

'Jerusalem, Jerusalem, you who kill the prophets and stone those sent to you, how often I have longed to gather your children together, as a hen gathers her chicks under her wings, and you were not willing. Look, your house is left to you desolate.'

The story is told that, after a fire on a farm, the body of a hen was found with her wings spread over her chicks to protect them. As Jesus, who came to seek and save the lost, looked out over the city, he longed to bring them all under his wings. Just like the mother hen, he would indeed spread out his arms on the cross, paying the price to save and protect his lost children.

This chapter, ending with Jesus' cry for Jerusalem, is taken up with a strong condemnation of the religious leaders: 'The teachers of the law and the Pharisees sit in Moses' seat. So you must be careful to do everything they tell you. But do not do what they do, for they do not practise what they preach' (vv. 2–3). Jesus accused them of public displays of holiness, of taking the most important seats, of hypocrisy and of making it more difficult for people to find the kingdom of heaven. They were fussy about tithing their spices, while neglecting justice and mercy.

These men knew the law: they read the Old Testament. They knew that God required justice and mercy; they knew the call to love both God and neighbour. They were revered and honoured by the people and they betrayed that trust. They had social and political as well as religious influence, and yet they ended up betraying Jesus to the Romans and forcing Pilate to execute him.

This chapter can seem somewhat irrelevant for us today. Yet all of us, especially those who have positions of influence, need to be aware that it is possible for our teaching and our example to make it hard for others to find the mercy of God.

....

Do we practise what we preach?

MK

The end of the world

'Keep watch, because you do not know on what day your Lord will come… If the owner of the house had known at what time of night the thief was coming, he would have kept watch… So you also must be ready, because the Son of Man will come at an hour when you do not expect him.'

This chapter is all about the future—but the question is 'What future?' and 'When…?' There have been many discussions about what future Jesus meant. Was he referring to his resurrection and ascension, to the destruction of the temple by the Roman army in AD70 or to the final ending, when he will come in glory as judge and there will be a new heaven and a new earth? Was he perhaps talking about all three? As we read this chapter, we can see the problems but we can also see an important truth for us all to take to heart: we need to be ready.

'Keep watch,' Jesus said, 'because you do not know on what day your Lord will come' (v. 42). The disciples were unprepared for the crucifixion and devastated by Jesus' death. They could not believe their eyes at first when he came back from the dead. When they did realise the truth of the resurrection, that he had indeed conquered death and paid the price for full forgiveness and new life in him, they were transformed to go out into the world with this wonderful gospel.

They also needed to be ready, though, to face war and devastation, famine and earthquakes, persecution, false prophets and false Messiahs—the distress of the times between Jesus' ascension and his return in glory, the times we are living in now.

Like the faithful and wise servant in Jesus' parable (vv. 45–51), we have to be ready for his return—tomorrow or in another thousand years. We need to be faithful in working to build his kingdom in the small corners of our lives, and wise as we deal with the distresses we and others face in our time.

....

The knowledge that we will, in the end, be gathered with all his saints in his glorious kingdom should fill us with an inner joy, however uncertain tomorrow may be.

MK

Well done, good and faithful servant

'When the Son of Man comes in his glory, and all the angels with him, he will sit on his glorious throne. All the nations will be gathered before him, and he will separate the people one from another as a shepherd separates the sheep from the goats.'

The three parables in this chapter all encourage us to be faithful and wise servants, who keep enough oil in their lamps, work hard to use their gifts and money to serve the king, and do their best to feed the hungry, welcome the stranger, look after the sick and visit the prisoner, especially when their own brothers and sisters in the faith are in need.

In these parables Jesus is encouraging his disciples, then and now, to do the work of the kingdom. How should we read them for ourselves today? As we read about the wedding attendants, we need to catch the excitement of the coming banquet. Jesus, our bridegroom, will return, and that promise should give us the deep sense of joy that is the fruit of his Spirit. But we need to be prepared for delay and not let that delay weaken our joy or our resolve to serve him.

How do we serve him? Sometimes we can find ourselves in two worlds. We worship and sing his praises with fellow believers on Sundays, carried away with the emotion of expressing our love for our Saviour, but what about Monday? Then we are a bit like the servants in Jesus' parable of the bags of gold (or 'talents' in some translations). We travel on the way to work or the shops, we take the children to school, drive to the tip, catch the train to a conference or plan a dinner party. Some of us are highly gifted, with responsible jobs and creative talents; others are a little more run-of-the-mill and some feel underused and at a loss. This is where we begin full-time, whole-life discipleship, making every bag of gold, every gift we have, work for the kingdom.

....

Learning to be whole-life disciples takes a lifetime as we bring everything under the Lordship of Christ—whether parenting, accounting, mountaineering or investing.

MK

On the way to the cross

But Peter declared, 'Even if I have to die with you, I will never disown you.' And all the other disciples said the same… Then [Peter] began to call down curses, and he swore to them, 'I don't know the man!' Immediately a cock crowed… And he went outside and wept bitterly.

Chapters 26 and 27 have over 60 verses each. They cover the crowded hours in Jerusalem from the last supper to the crucifixion and burial of Jesus, and they are filled with significant events for Peter and Judas, high priest Caiaphas and Pontius Pilate, the Roman governor, as well as the crowds and the soldiers. Over Easter we will hear these events at church, read and sung, but I would love to encourage you to sit down in a quiet place and read through these two chapters, perhaps imagining yourself as one of the disciples.

At one level these are ordinary events—meals with friends, hustle and bustle, plotting and fear, brave words and miserable betrayal, prayer in the face of deep trouble, and an armed mob sent by political leaders. We know that such things are happening even now, somewhere in the world. Yet, in truth, this is the most significant, amazing, pivotal event in the history of human beings—in the history of creation from beginning to end. God so loved the world that he sent his Son to drink the cup of God's wrath so that anyone who believes in him shall have everlasting life, full forgiveness and a place at his side in eternity.

As Jesus accepts everything that he has to suffer, we watch all the other people in these chapters demonstrating why they need repentance and forgiveness. Peter, so sure of his love and loyalty, probably did not understand what was going on; even so, he wanted to stay beside the Lord he loved, whatever the consequences. But Jesus knew his weakness, the cock crowed and Peter, like all of us, had to face the bitterness of what he had done.

....

May Gethsemane drive us all to our knees, knowing that we too have been among the scoffers and the betrayers.

MK

The power of the cross

When the centurion and those with him… saw the earthquake and all that had happened, they were terrified, and exclaimed, 'Surely he was the Son of God!' Many women were there, watching from a distance. They had followed Jesus from Galilee to care for his needs.

In all the mayhem and terror, some behaved badly—Judas, Peter and the other disciples; Pilate, giving in to the mob; soldiers ill-treating a helpless and stricken victim; priests and elders standing round a dying man to mock and taunt him. But now it is done. Jesus is dead, and, as far as most of his followers are concerned, that is the tragic and disappointing end of a great adventure.

When the hurricane has passed, when the bombardment has stopped, when silence descends over an earthquake-stricken town, some people come out of hiding to see how they can help the injured, the bereaved and the lost. Human beings can do dreadful things but they can also try to comfort, to give what little they can.

There were onlookers on that hill of death who offered Jesus a drink; the centurion, overwhelmed by the darkness and the earthquake, acknowledged that there was something about Jesus he did not understand. And the women were there, including his mother. It was all they could do: they kept watch at the cross, they followed his body to the tomb and they kept watch until the sabbath was over. There was Joseph of Arimathea, perhaps a scared secret disciple, who bravely went to Pilate for permission to bury the body. Maybe Pilate's conscience was troubling him and this was the least he could do.

It is hard when there is little we can do about other people's difficult situations—a terminal illness, a child astray, unfair dismissal from work, a repossessed home—except watch and pray. In the aftermath, however, we may find a place to comfort, cook, open our home or simply be there.

....

Do you know anyone to whom bad things have happened, who has no hope? Pray, watch, and do what you can for them.

Read 2 Corinthians 1:3–7 for more about being comforted and comforting.

MK

Get going

Then Jesus came to them and said, '… Go and make disciples of all nations, baptising them in the name of the Father and of the Son and of the Holy Spirit, and teaching them to obey everything I have commanded you. And surely I am with you always, to the very end of the age.'

What does the resurrection of Jesus mean for us today? Many have argued that it was a figment of the disciples' imagination. Perhaps, in their traumatic distress at his death, they sensed his presence and thought they saw him. But Jesus went out of his way to convince them that he was fully himself, a physical presence in this world in which he died. He ate fish for breakfast with them (John 21:12); he showed his wounds to Thomas (John 20:27); he appeared to the disciples and the women several times, and, according to Paul, he appeared to 'more than five hundred of the brothers and sisters at the same time' (1 Corinthians 15:6). When we say, 'I believe in the resurrection of the body', it is not just about Jesus coming back from the dead as himself, a transformed but recognisable person. We too, in the same way, will live one day as transformed individuals in a newly recreated earth, his restored kingdom.

Matthew's message is that the kingdom of God began when Jesus came. He called his disciples to be kingdom people, living out the way of the kingdom until he comes back. So his final message to us all, as he ascends to the throne of his Father, is 'Get going!' This command is not just about evangelism or crosscultural mission. It is a command to each one of us, wherever we are, to bring the justice and joy, reconciliation and love of his kingdom into his world. It is also about making disciples, and that means planting churches, forming fellowships into which new disciples are baptised and where we and they learn to obey everything he has commanded.

....

Read Jesus' last command again—then get going!

MK

Rosemary Green introduces the next two weeks' readings.

My father died when I was a baby (I didn't see him after I was two months old) and my mother was shy and reserved. For very many years as a Christian, I found it hard to be deeply sure of God's love. I went to pray with a friend as I sought to know God's love for myself. Nothing seemed to change. Then one day, apparently out of the blue, something happened that enabled me to say, 'Now I've felt God's love, and I can stop worrying about it.' I have forgotten what the 'something' was—quite small and, of itself, insignificant—but it was enough to bring a new assurance of the Father's love.

It is even harder for a person who has had an abusive human father to know God as Father; many Christians shy away from the idea altogether. If a slide projector gets two slides stuck in together, two images are projected on to the screen simultaneously. The biblical image of a good, loving God can be superimposed on the image of an abusive, inconsistent father; the image from experience, planted first and deeply rooted in the emotions, seems far stronger. We cannot change the confusion by ourselves but, if we really want the biblical image to predominate, it can happen. Our choice plus prayer and the Holy Spirit lead to new belief, new trust and new experience.

One vital key to eradicating the old image is our willingness to forgive those who have caused it. So in these readings we look first at a psalm, to refute the often-held idea that the Old Testament God is harsh and exacting while the New Testament God is soft and loving. Then, after thinking more about God's character, we read how Jesus related to his Father and see how we can relate to our heavenly Father.

Some books you might find helpful are *Knowing God* by J.I. Packer (the chapter on 'Sons of God'), *The Shack* by William P. Young, *The Forgotten Father* by Tom Smail and *The Father Heart of God* by Floyd McClung.

A God who is good

As the heavens are high above the earth, so great is his steadfast love towards those who fear him; as far as the east is from the west, so far he removes our transgressions from us. As a father has compassion for his children, so the Lord has compassion for those who fear him.

I have a soft spot for this psalm: we had part of it read in our wedding service over 50 years ago. I chose it for today's reading because it knocks away the common misconception that the God of the Old Testament is a vindictive, unjust God while the God of the New Testament is a God of love. So we start our readings on the fatherhood of God in the Old Testament, in this psalm where David expresses how he experiences God's utter goodness and wants to praise this God with his whole being.

David's God heals, rescues, satisfies, renews and reveals himself. He works justice for those who are treated unjustly; he is a God of steadfast love and mercy. In that love and mercy, he forgives. David had reason to need and to know God's forgiveness after his adultery with Bathsheba and his plans to ensure the death in battle of her husband Uriah. (We find this story in 2 Samuel 11—12.) Verses 9–12 show how sure he was that God forgives. I am glad, though, that David does not ignore God's anger. A holy, just God cannot ignore our wrongdoing but his righteous anger gives way to his steadfast love and mercy. A friend of mine was a fighter pilot in World War II. He told me how he thought of verse 12 in the cockpit of his plane, seeing the immense distance from one horizon to the other: 'so far he removes our transgressions from us'. The compassionate Father wants us to be sure that he really does forgive all our iniquity.

'Do not forget all his benefits' (v. 2). Make a list of all the 'benefits' you have received from God. Then praise him!

Read Psalm 51:1–17 to see the depth of David's contrition and of his plea for forgiveness.

RG

A welcoming Father

'While he was still a long way off, his father saw him and was filled with compassion for him; he ran to his son, threw his arms around him and kissed him.'

A young man had been in prison for many years. Before he was due for release, he wrote home to say that he would be returning by bus on a particular day. If he was welcome, would they hang a yellow ribbon on the tree outside the house? As the bus passed the house, he would look out. If there was a ribbon, he would alight; no ribbon, and he would continue on his way. As the bus approached his home, he hardly dared look, and asked the person sitting next to him to tell him what he saw. There wasn't just one ribbon on the tree—it was festooned in yellow! He knew he was welcome.

What a great illustration of the well-known parable Jesus told! The young man in Jesus' story had made a mess of his life and he finally realised it. He started his journey home, humbly, perhaps scared at the reception he might get, but 'while he was still a long way off, his father saw him'. The implication is that, despite his long absence, his father was still looking out for him. Then came the welcome, the fine clothes, the celebration, the lavish party and the father's joy. Yes, if we stray from God's path, whether in selfish disobedience or through careless mistakes, we need to come back in humble repentance, and we can be sure of his loving welcome.

The father's joy was marred by the grudging attitude of the dutiful older son, who knew more about rules than about relationship. God has his rules but relationship matters more. We sometimes get our perspective wrong. The Father longs for us to be secure in his love and to respond to him in love.

....

Father, please help me to be sure of your welcoming love, even when I know I do not deserve it.

Read Matthew 6:14–15 and think about how the two sons, the Father and yourself fit with these verses.

RG

God's greatest gifts

'I will ask the Father, and he will give you another Counsellor to be with you for ever—the Spirit of truth… The Counsellor, the Holy Spirit, whom the Father will send in my name, will teach you all things and will remind you of everything I have said to you.'

The disciples were scared. They had enjoyed his friendship, his teaching and his ministry. They realised that he was preparing to leave them and they were afraid to be on their own. So Jesus told them about the great gift the Father would give them and us—the gift of the Holy Spirit, who would be their Counsellor and companion for ever. He is the Spirit of truth who teaches us. He lives with us and in us.

The Spirit is one of the two greatest gifts the Father gives us. The other is his Son, Jesus. Probably the best-known verse in the Bible is John 3:16: 'For God so loved the world that he gave his one and only Son, that whoever believes in him should not perish but have eternal life.' Nothing demonstrates the Father's love for us more clearly than the gift of his Son to die for us (see Romans 5:8). I have been a Christian for nearly 60 years and I pray that I may never grow blasé about that truth.

It was 8 October 1950 when I realised that Jesus' death on the cross was for me because I was a sinner and I needed his forgiveness. Twenty-four hours later I invited his Spirit into my life, but for many years I kept that Spirit of Christ confined to the living-room of the house of my life. It took me another 24 years to allow him to roam freely and take control of the whole house. I had changed in those first 24 years, but nothing like as much as I have changed since then. I rejoice in the Father's gifts of the Son and the Spirit, and pray that I will continue to grow in grace and in likeness to Christ until I die.

....

Father, thank you that you love us so much that you gave us your Son to die for us and your Spirit to live in us.

RG

A Father to be trusted

'Do not worry, saying, "What shall we eat?" or "What shall we drink?" or "What shall we wear?" For the pagans run after all these things, and your heavenly Father knows that you need them. But seek first his kingdom and his righteousness, and all these things will be given to you as well.'

My life was in turmoil so I decided to read the book of Job, hoping it would help in my perplexity. It did—eventually! Much of the book confused me. What was truth and what was half-truth in the comments made by Job and his friends? Finally I found Job saying in 42:2, 'I know that you can do all things; no plan of yours can be thwarted.' That verse leapt off the page. It seemed that God himself had hammered a solid post into the ground. He is the God who makes no mistakes. I saw that there is no point in trusting a God who is right only 98 per cent of the time. He is a God who is 100 per cent trustworthy.

Jesus told his listeners that they had no cause to worry about their basic needs. Their heavenly Father, who feeds the birds and beautifies the flowers, cares even more for his children. But how does that square, we ask, with those who lose jobs and homes in the economic downturn or for those who face starvation in Ethiopia? Is he really the 100 per cent trustworthy Father for them? It is easy to blame God and say that he does not keep his promises—'but seek first the kingdom of God and his righteousness'. Selfishness, greed, a lust for power and many other human sins obstruct the free flow of the word's resources. It is not God's fault that the world is in such a mess.

This brings me to a number of questions. Do I trust a heavenly Father who provides my basic needs, not necessarily everything I desire? Do I do even my little bit to conserve the world's resources? Do I give to those who have less than I do? Do I seek the kingdom of God and his righteousness?

....

Father, please help me to be sure that you really are to be trusted at all times, and show me how I can seek and advance your kingdom on earth.

RG

The unique Son

'Don't you believe that I am in the Father, and that the Father is in me? The words I say to you are not just my own. Rather, it is the Father, living in me, who is doing his work.'

In these readings on the Fatherhood of God, we want to see how Jesus—living on earth as a human being, dependent on his Father—can be a model for us in our relationship as children with the Father. At the same time we realise that our relationship with the Father cannot be exactly the same as his. Jesus the Son is unique, and his relationship with the Father is unique, because he, 'God's one and only Son' (John 3:18), *is* God. 'I and my Father are one,' Jesus said on another occasion (John 10:30). This was one of many things that infuriated the Jews and roused their desire to kill him: 'he was even calling God his own Father, making himself equal with God' (John 5:18).

I confess that I find it easier to fall into the heresy of thinking of the Godhead as three separate beings who relate closely to one another than to grasp the unity of the Trinity, of three Persons in one God. But 'I am in the Father and the Father is in me,' says our reading today (v. 11). Jesus and his Father (yes, and the Holy Spirit, too) are bound up inextricably as one in a unique relationship. (If you have read the novel *The Shack* you will remember how the author brings home in an unusual way the quality of relationship in the Trinity.) The divine nature makes them one. Jesus' Sonship is unique. Yet the incarnate Jesus, who 'made himself nothing, taking the very nature of a servant, being made in human likeness' (Philippians 2:7), shows us how we can relate to our heavenly Father in prayer, in obedience, in character, in trust, even in suffering—at the same time as he, the unique Son, shows us what the Father is like.

....

God, please help me, through your Spirit at work in me, to understand more about Jesus' relationship with the Father.

Read Hebrews 1:1–4 to see the Son's uniqueness.

RG

The privilege of adoption

You have received a spirit of adoption. When we cry, 'Abba! Father!' it is that very Spirit bearing witness with our spirit that we are children of God, and if children, then heirs, heirs of God and joint heirs with Christ.

Adopted by God! What a privilege! Think what adoption means in our society. Situations vary, but in each case a child is in an underprivileged situation, where the natural parents cannot care properly for that child. The child is brought into a new home and given the rights and privileges of being a full member of a new family. We who are Christians have the rights and privileges of being full members of God's family, heirs of God, with all the riches of his inheritance to claim (astonishingly, alongside the unique Son). That is fantastic! One of those privileges is to call him, 'Abba! Father!' We can use the name of the Father that Jesus used when he prayed; we can have confidence in our access to the Father. That, too, is amazing.

There are two things I specially want to notice in this reading. One is the common misconception that all people are God's children. That is not true. We are all his creation (even though that creation has been spoilt) but we are not all automatically his children. That privilege is for those who receive Christ's Spirit and follow him, who come from outside his family to be adopted into his family. Notice, too, where the parallel of human adoption falls short. Adopting parents may or may not know about the child's genes but, however carefully they teach and train the child, they cannot change its DNA. God's adoption goes one better. We read in the New Testament of 'new birth' and a 'new nature'. The very DNA of our character can be changed as the Holy Spirit who comes to give us new life gradually changes us, and our marred character becomes more like our Father's.

....

Father, I pray that I may have confidence in my status as your adopted child, but that I may never take it for granted or become blasé about the privilege.

RG

God's X-ray eyes

O Lord, you have searched me and you know me. You know when I sit down and when I rise; you perceive my thoughts from afar… If I say, 'Surely the darkness will hide me and the light become night around me,' even the darkness will not be dark to you.

'Big Brother is watching you'—with the ever-increasing use of CCTV cameras. God is watching us, too. I used to be scared of his X-ray eyes. I felt uncomfortable and ashamed that he knew everything going on inside me, that no dark corner was hidden from his penetrating gaze. Like Adam and Eve in the garden of Eden, I wanted to hide—but there was nowhere to go. Then at some point I realised that my fear had been replaced by a sense of security. I cannot remember exactly when it happened but I believe it was connected with my realisation that God really is a heavenly Father who loves me, forgives me and wants the best for me, not a stern judge who will condemn me for all my faults.

My feelings changed. Instead of wanting to retreat, I am now glad he knows everything that is going on inside me. As it is said, 'He knows the worst about me and loves me just the same.' For the psalmist, too, God's all-seeing eye was a cause for security and joy, not fear. 'Such knowledge is too wonderful for me' (v. 6); 'your hand will guide me, your right hand will hold me fast' (v. 10); 'how precious to me are your thoughts' (v. 17). He felt safe with this God who knew him through and through.

This psalm does not specifically talk of God as Father, so you might say that it does not fit in with this series of readings, but this God who watches, who sees right inside us, is not an X-ray machine. He is one who loves us, holds us, wants our best and cares for us as a good father does—and we should fear him with the fear that respects, not the fear that is afraid.

....

Can you pray verses 23 and 24 of Psalm 139 for yourself? Try it, even if you want to tell him that you are scared at the same time as wanting to feel safe with him.

RG

Modelling the Father

I kneel before the Father, from whom all fatherhood in heaven and on earth derives its name… I pray that you, being rooted and grounded in love, may have power, together with all the saints, to grasp how wide and long and high and deep is the love of Christ, and to know this love that surpasses knowledge.

Today is Fathers' Day, so we focus on the NIV's alternative translation for verse 14: 'the Father, from whom all fatherhood derives its name.' It is no mistake that God is called Father, for the parent–child relationship springs from God and should model what God is like. I say 'parent', because female as well as male characteristics are bound up in God's personality. Fatherhood—parenthood—is a joy (however exasperating or disappointing our children may be at times). It is a great privilege and a great responsibility. I once knew a man who saw God as an unapproachable father hidden behind his newspaper; this man's own father (a Christian) had little real relationship with his children, so his God was distant and he felt himself a failure.

Recently I met a doctor who wrote this: 'Because of her own background, my mother was unable to deal with emotions at all, whether to share, encourage, explore, or direct them. I have no memory of ever being kissed or cuddled, and had my first birthday party after being married.' He knew in his head but knew nothing in his heart of God's love until God intervened in a surprising and dramatic way. A medical mistake that he made might have cost a patient her sight, but God spoke directly to him: 'The reason I am restoring this woman's sight is not for her sake but for yours, because I want you to know how much I love you.' This doctor's attitude to his surroundings, to his wife and children and to God started to change as he learnt the reality of God's love for him.

....

Make Ephesians 3:16–19 your prayer for yourself or anyone else you know and care about: 'I pray that he may strengthen me/Dad/John/Jane with power through his spirit in my/his/her inner being…' and so on.

RG

Close to his Father

Jesus… looked toward heaven and prayed: 'Father, the time has come. Glorify your Son, that your Son may glorify you… Father, glorify me in your presence with the glory I had with you before the world began.'

Throughout his ministry we find Jesus keeping in touch with his Father. We are told that he prayed at his baptism when God affirmed him as his beloved Son (Luke 3:21–23); early in the morning after a long, hard day (Mark 1:35); for a whole night before choosing the Twelve (Luke 6:12); publicly before feeding the five thousand (Mark 6:41) and in private afterwards (v. 46); by Lazarus' grave (John 11:41); after 72 of his disciples returned from their mission (Luke 10:21–22); during the last week of his life, with some Greeks who had come to Jerusalem for the Passover (John 12:28); in the garden of Gethsemane, as he faced the greatest test of his life (Luke 22:42); on the cross as he prayed forgiveness for those who crucified him (23:34) and as he died (v. 46). Those are just the occasions the Gospel writers tell us about, and, whenever we are told the words he used, his prayer was addressed to his Father. We might say that constant communion with his Father was his lifeblood, in times set apart for prayer in a private place as well as in public ministry.

Those incidents give us snatches of Jesus at prayer, but his extended prayer in John 17 (the 'high priestly prayer', as it is known) shows the intimacy of the union between the Son and the Father. His crucifixion was imminent—the death that would complete all he came to do on earth. That ultimate expression of the love of the Father and Son for human beings would bring glory to God, however shameful a death it looked to human onlookers, and he could pray verse 5 with confidence, knowing that his rightful place was to be exalted at the Father's right hand.

....

Jesus continued to pray for his disciples and for all believers. We can enter into his prayer by praying for ourselves and for other Christian believers, adapting his words to use as our own.

RG

Lord, teach us to pray

'When you pray, say: "Father, hallowed be your name, your kingdom come. Give us each day our daily bread. Forgive us our sins, for we also forgive everyone who sins against us. And lead us not into temptation."'

The disciples watched Jesus talking with his Father. They could see that the relationship was something special, and they wanted it for themselves. Jesus told them they were to pray to God as Father, just as he did. I guess that thrilled them! Do you have the same hunger for intimacy with our Father? I confess that my hunger is patchy. I often rush into prayer, then rush out again to the next activity. An Anglican nun told me that she takes 20 minutes to 'centre in' on God before being ready for any other aspects of prayer. We need to take time for adoration if we are to grow in intimacy with the Father.

I like the story of a small boy who threw his favourite toy down in anger and broke it. Johnny spent a miserable day. When his father returned from work, the little boy showed him the broken toy: 'Daddy, I'm sorry I was cross. Please will you mend it?' They went into Daddy's workshop. As he watched his father at work, Johnny said, 'Daddy, aren't you wonderful!' The repaired toy was handed back: 'Thank you, Daddy.' Sorry, please and thank you: those are often the easiest aspects of prayer. Adoration—'Aren't you wonderful!'—worships the unseen Father for who he is.

Read Luke 11:9–13 again and see God's goodness and generosity. Read verses 5–8: God wants us to persevere when we don't see an immediate answer. Then pray slowly the prayer Jesus taught us, not as one prayer but using each phrase as a heading for other thoughts and prayers. 'Father, hallowed be your name... Your kingdom come... Give us each day our daily bread... forgive us our sins... for we also forgive everyone... Lead us not into temptation...'

....

Jesus invites us to come to him as little children. What are your 'sorry', 'please' and 'thank you' prayers to bring to him today?

RG

'I always please him'

Going a little farther, he fell with his face to the ground and prayed, 'My Father, if it is possible, may this cup be taken from me. Yet not as I will, but as you will.'

Throughout his life, Jesus was intent on pleasing his Father: 'My food is to do the will of him who sent me and to finish his work' (John 4:34); 'I have come down from heaven not to do my own will but to do the will of him that sent me' (6:38); 'I always do what pleases him' (8:29); 'I do exactly what my Father has commanded me' (14:31). We see this attitude of obedience—an obedience born of love for a loving Father—supremely in the garden of Gethsemane. Jesus was facing the biggest test of his life, and he was afraid. It was not primarily the fear of the physical agony of crucifixion, or of the emotional pain of disappointment—disappointment with the failures of his friends or the anticipation of their disappointment when their high hopes in him would be dashed. The biggest agony for Jesus would be carrying the load of the world's sin. As Paul wrote later, 'God made him who had no sin to be sin for us' (2 Corinthians 5:21). That was an almost intolerable burden for the holy Son. He who had always been in touch with his Father would be cut off from him: remember his anguished cry, 'My God, my God, why have you forsaken me?' (Matthew 27:46).

No wonder Jesus was afraid of the next 24 hours, so his prayer in the garden was intense: 'My Father, if it is possible, may this cup [of suffering] be taken from me.' But he wanted to fulfil his commission on earth. He wanted to please his Father, so he was ready to leave the garden and face his enemies.

....

Father, thank you that it was for the world's sake, and it was for my sake, that Jesus' desire to please his Father took him to the cross.

RG

The obedience of love

'As the Father has loved me, so have I loved you. Now remain in my love. If you obey my commands, you will remain in my love, just as I have obeyed my Father's commands and remain in his love.'

Years ago I learnt a hard but vital lesson about the danger of disobeying God. In May one year, he warned me that a close friendship was out of proportion; I needed to straighten it out. 'Yes, Lord, I will—in September, when the church year starts up again.' Before September, though, that friendship crashed, setting off one of the most painful, humiliating periods of my life—from which I emerged as a new, stronger person.

I had learnt an important lesson: the folly of disobeying God; the folly even of procrastinating. If the Father tells me to do something, he means now, not later. I saw clearly a simple truth: if God loves me, he wants the best for me. That is logical. If he is all wisdom, he knows what is best for me. That's logical, too. Well, if he wants my best and knows what's best, what's the point of disobeying him? The sequence seems simplistic, but when I grasped it, it changed my attitude to obeying God. Instead of arguing with him, it became natural to want to please him. What is more, if he is all-powerful, his Spirit's power is available to help me do what may seem difficult. Obeying a Father who knows me and loves me became a new joy and brought new freedom in my life—a reality, not a pious platitude.

Read verses 9–11 again: '… that your joy may be complete'. Yes, it's true, and if we know that God's love for us is real, then that love can be planted in us. So loving other people becomes easier than it used to be, despite their irritating habits—because it is the Father's love growing in us, the love that enables him to love us despite all the ways we grieve him.

....

'Trust and obey, for there's no other way to be happy in Jesus but to trust and obey.' (John Henry Sammis, 1846–1919)

Read 1 John 2:3–6 and reflect on what John had learnt in his old age.

RG

It's for your own good

My child, do not regard lightly the discipline of the Lord, or lose heart when you are punished by him; for the Lord disciplines those whom he loves, and chastises every child whom he accepts.

'It's for your own good... This hurts me more than it hurts you.' What child really believes those words when the heavy hand of parental discipline falls? Those comments are occasionally true, if the punishment really does fit the crime and if the parent is genuinely grieved that it is needed, but I remember with shame how often my children's small misdemeanours triggered an explosion of anger. The wrath I vented was totally disproportionate, entirely unjustified and was certainly not for the child's good. Even when I apologised later, that did not undo the damage I had done or the fear I had inculcated. It is not necessarily true that we respect the human parents who discipline us (see verse 9).

God's discipline of his children is not like that. He really does 'discipline us for our good'. Why? 'In order that we may share his holiness' (v. 10). He is not looking for our external conformity to his rules, but for the re-creation of our character, of which Paul wrote in 2 Corinthians 5:17: 'If anyone is in Christ, there is a new creation.'

Furthermore, discipline does not mean only punishment. It may be done by example, by making rules and setting boundaries, training and teaching what is right as well as rebuking what is wrong. Jesus disciplined his followers by his example and his teaching, by his own ministry and by sending them out into ministry. Yes, he rebuked them too, sometimes in no uncertain terms. 'Get behind me, Satan! You are a stumbling-block to me' were strong words to Peter when he refused to believe Jesus' warning about his coming death at the hands of the Jewish leaders (Matthew 16:23). I am sure Peter never forgot that lesson in listening to Jesus and believing him.

....

Thank you, heavenly Father, that your discipline really is for my good. I pray that I may recognise your discipline, submit to it gladly and be changed through it.

RG

The privilege of suffering

If we are children, then we are heirs—heirs of God and co-heirs with Christ, if indeed we share in his sufferings in order that we may also share in his glory. I consider that our present sufferings are not worth comparing with the glory that will be revealed in us.

We read most of these verses a week ago when we rejoiced in the tremendous privilege of being adopted into God's family, but we overlooked one clause: '… if indeed we share in his sufferings in order that we may also share in his glory'. There was no short cut for Jesus. He had to go through the valley of the cross before he could reap the mountaintop triumph of the resurrection and ascension. The way led through suffering to glory for him, and that is the way for us: it is one aspect of the privilege of being a child of God.

We will all suffer in some way, some more than others, and hardship always changes us. It may lead to hardness and bitterness or it can lead to refinement and growth, a deeper knowledge of what it means to be a child of God and co-heir with Christ. Two of the biggest blessings of my life came through suffering. Through my husband's serious illness in South Africa (over which I had no control), the Holy Spirit revived my waning spirituality and gave me a new love for Jesus. Later, through painful events brought about by my own explosive wrath (for which I was responsible), my anger was rooted out and I emerged as a cleaner, more confident person.

Our heavenly Father may not choose all our suffering but he allows it. When events in our lives do not go the way we would have chosen, we can either complain that he isn't concerned for us or we can go back to the beginning of these readings. Is he altogether good? Does he love us and forgive us? Is he totally trustworthy? Then we can ask for his help to go through the valley, holding on to the hand of Jesus, who has been that way before.

....

Father, please help me to trust you, whatever troubles may come in my life.

Read Philippians 3:10 to see Paul's deepest desire in his life.

RG

Chris Leonard introduces the theme we will be focusing on for the next two weeks.

We need names to understand someone or something. For example, in 1802, Englishman Luke Howard was the first to name types of cloud and work out what each one meant in terms of rain, wind and so on. Meteorologists still use his names and classifications every day to understand and forecast the weather.

As for the right name, we struggle to name organisations, clubs, outreach events and books—let alone children. Suppose you'd been called 'Margaret Thatcher' or 'Rose West' before those perfectly ordinary names became famous or infamous? What names are you known by? Do you like them? Have you changed them? Would you?

Have you been called gifted, stupid, lazy? Coward, sexy, unhelpful? Fun, teacher's pet, clumsy, skinny? Kind, disgusting, idiot, a true friend? What 'names' do you call other people? What effect does your naming have on them?

By what name does God call you? John 10:3 says, 'He calls his own sheep by name and leads them out.' Has he ever renamed you, as he did with several Bible characters? He will do, according to Revelation 2:17.

We rate names mainly by sound and association but biblical names reveal foundational truth about identity, and we'll explore that. Over the next two weeks we'll see what the Bible has to say about our names, including the extraordinarily good news that God knows each one of his people by name, allows us to pray and to act in his name, and even gives us his name. Do search the scriptures and read around the subject when you've time. Each name reveals something different about the character involved.

What's in a name?

'You are to give him the name Jesus, because he will save his people from their sins.' All this took place to fulfil what the Lord had said through the prophet: 'The virgin will… give birth to a son, and they will call him Immanuel'—which means, 'God with us.'

Do you like your names? My given names are Christine Mary, which are OK, I suppose. They're very 'Christian': 'of Christ' plus the name of his mother, chosen because I arrived just before Christmas. Chris*tine* still carries the ring of childhood disapproval with it, so I prefer Chris. I use Mary only on official documents. I was pleased to be rid of the surname 'Williams' on marriage and move up the alphabet to the less ubiquitous, if oddly spelled, 'Leonard'.

Today we judge names not by meaning but by sound; initials are important, too. So are associations with people we like or dislike. Psychologist Dr David Holmes' recent research purports to show that women called Judy are happiest, because of positive associations with Judi Dench or Judy Finnegan, while Paulines are unhappy because of Pauline Fowler in *EastEnders*. Dear, dear, what have we come to? Do we really treat Paulines so badly by association, making them unhappy?

Joseph's angel-dream about the naming of his fiancée's son follows a long list of names: Joseph's genealogy in Matthew 1 goes right back to Adam. Some of those names we know well; others appear here but nowhere else in the Bible. Clearly names and their 'owners'—are important to God! The name 'Jesus' is a form of 'Joshua', which means 'God is my salvation'. Even more than the first Joshua, Jesus was to save his people from their sins, and be called 'God with us'. Imagine carrying that responsibility, those associations along with your name, from birth! Because he lived up to it, all the way, there is power in the name of Jesus.

....

Praise him! Ask him to be speaking to you about any issues with your names and their associations—or with the official and unofficial names you've given others.

CL

Deriving your family name

For this reason I kneel before the Father, from whom his whole family in heaven and on earth derives its name. I pray that out of his glorious riches he may strengthen you with power through his Spirit in your inner being, so that Christ may dwell in your hearts through faith.

I'm fascinated by Paul's implied genealogy in this passage. How can the Father's whole family derive its name from him? Scientists speak of a genetic 'first mother' to whom we can all be traced, but surely no families, human or angelic, are named 'Father' or 'God'?

Have you tried tracing your ancestors? The number of people who share my birth-family name, Williams, makes it difficult to research. Nevertheless, according to family tradition, our ancestry through my father's mother's father's mother (I hope you're following!) goes back to Robin of Locksley, aka Robin Hood. Impressive, eh? Or hard to believe! Now, through the vast resources of the Internet, I'm assured by many also related to Thomas de Lokesley (c. 1330–1417, Bailiff of Bradfield) that he's the connection and that our hero's shenanigans took place near Sheffield rather than Nottingham. No one I've known in my family seems anything like Robin Hood, though: swashbucklers we're not!

I love TV programmes that help a well-known person trace their ancestry. Usually the subjects want to find out why they are like they are—but it's striking how seldom the lifestyle and personalities uncovered connect with their own. Ah, now we're getting somewhere. In biblical times, the name expressed a person's nature and character. No matter to whom we're related, if we act, pray and live 'in the name of' the Father, Son and Holy Spirit, we'll derive our true name, our character and personality, from them. We'll be rooted and established in their love, 'filled to the measure of all the fullness of God' (v. 19). Also, we're adopted into the Father's family. That sure beats Robin Hood. What a family, what ancestry, what a name!

....

'Now to him who is able to do immeasurably more than all we ask or imagine, according to his power that is at work within us, to him be glory in the church and in Christ Jesus throughout all generations, for ever and ever! Amen' (Ephesians 3:20–21).

CL

Making a name for yourselves?

They came upon a plain in Shinar and settled there… Then they said, 'Come, let us build ourselves a city, and a tower with its top in the heavens, and let us make a name for ourselves; otherwise we shall be scattered upon the face of the whole earth.'

It's not a bad thing, to make a name for ourselves. Build a spectacular tower: that'll make anyone who even thinks about attacking us think again. We'll stick together and work hard, even making our own building materials. Independence and self-sufficiency as a group, strength, strategic planning, initiative, teamwork—we'd win *The Apprentice* with no one being fired.

It wasn't Sir Alan Sugar, however, but the Lord who came down to see what these early Babylonians had built—and he wasn't happy. Why? We can work it out from later in the Bible. Proverbs 18:10 says, 'The name of the Lord is a strong tower; the righteous run into it and are safe.' Hebrews 12 says that the only city that cannot be shaken is 'the city of the living God, the heavenly Jerusalem' (vv. 22, 28).

Translated into the 21st century, the Bible shows up the nonsense of our reliance on weapons of mass destruction and our trust in 'free market economies'. Look what a mess such things have got us into! We were never meant to make a name for ourselves: God longs to give us glorious names. We're not meant to be independent in terms of defence and provision but to rely on God. How much trouble that would save!

It's not easy when we're stuck in the systems of government policies, global economics and complex defence treaties, but we'd better learn fast to grasp the concept when those systems break down. Everything that the ancient tower-builders feared came upon them: having confused their communication, God scattered them all over the earth. I wonder if that severe mercy caused any to turn to him.

Read Ephesians 6:10–19, considering what it might mean to pray in the Spirit, standing firm against the 'principalities and powers'. Could those powers include the corrupt mega-systems on this earth? How might we proclaim God's name to them?

CL

Known by name

'Woman,' he said, 'why are you crying? Who is it you are looking for?' Thinking he was the gardener, she said, 'Sir, if you have carried him away, tell me where you have put him, and I will get him.' Jesus said to her, 'Mary.' She turned toward him and cried out in Aramaic, 'Rabboni!' (which means Teacher).

Jesus said, 'The sheep listen to [the shepherd's] voice. He calls his own sheep by name and leads them out' (John 10:3). By what name, or names, does he call you? He calls me 'Child' mainly, which could sound impersonal but it's spoken with such love—and, as I'm now 55, it brings welcome reassurance that I'm not too grown-up to be in his kingdom. Maybe he calls you 'My beloved' or 'My beautiful one, who has ravished my heart!' What he will never call you are names like 'Worthless', 'Soiled', 'Unwelcome', 'Dismissed'.

The risen Jesus called Mary by her given name. So many of the women he knew shared that name. It means 'bitter' and, although Jesus had long seen past that label, all the Marys close to him experienced the bitterest of times the day he died, and the next. But early on Sunday morning, as Jesus spoke her name, Mary Magdalene, who loved him much because she'd been forgiven much, saw through her tears her beloved Jesus. She saw an end to the bitter grief that had destroyed her past, present and future. She heard pure love and, as her world started singing, she spoke her special name for him: 'Rabboni' or 'Teacher'. What a moving, intimate, joy-dazzling moment.

Now *we* are in an intimate relationship with God—Father, Son and Holy Spirit. Isn't that amazing? What are your special names for him? He knows each one of us by name. He knows completely what we are like, bad as well as good, and yet we hear him call our names with such anticipation, such love. We know him by name, call on his name, run to him as Mary did.

....

Listen now, as you would for a lover, for him to call your name.
Enjoy some intimate time together—for nothing but good can flow
from such a time.

CL

Our ministry of naming

The Lord God formed every animal of the field and every bird of the air, and brought them to the man to see what he would call them; and whatever the man called each living creature, that was its name.

Suppose *Day by Day with God* were called *Engineering Theorems* or *Satanism for Beginners*? Would you buy or read it? Shakespeare said, 'A rose by any other name would smell as sweet', but certain names lack appeal: they wouldn't 'sell' the book or would so mislead buyers about the content that they would read only a few words.

If I 'create' something—a book, for example—I like either to name it myself or to be given the chance to approve its title. I certainly wouldn't have wanted anyone naming a baby of mine—apart from my husband, and then as a joint effort. Yet, here is God, having created this brand new planet, allowing the very first human being to name all his astounding new creatures. Free will—what grace, what risk! God makes, then Adam names and identifies with, Woman— and in the next chapter Adam blames her for leading him astray.

However you interpret the truth of the creation stories, God goes on allowing humankind to 'name' his creatures—to decide on their identity. Which will be useful beasts of burden or much-loved companions, and which will be despised or feared? Often we name wrongly or abusively—breaking the patient donkey's back, abusing the defenceless giant turtle, dressing up the chimps, fearing non-poisonous spiders while fighting giant whales or fierce tigers to show that we can. Our misunderstanding (misnaming) of God's creatures brings conflict as we fail to respect their natures and needs, destroying their habitats through our selfish greed. We've not cared for them as we would for an object that we'd 'created' and named ourselves.

Worst of all, we rename parts of the human race. That leads to exploitation, racism, sexism, ageism, war, holocaust and more.

....

Lord, you want us to love, care, create, learn and enjoy—and to name well. Forgive all our abuses. May your will be done on earth, as it is in heaven.

CL

Naming and renaming

The first thing Andrew did was to find his brother Simon and tell him, 'We have found the Messiah' (that is, the Christ). And he brought him to Jesus. Jesus looked at him and said, 'You are Simon son of John. You will be called Cephas' (which, when translated, is Peter).

'You're misunderstood by many, including your church, but God sees the work you're doing and it's beautiful.' So prayed a woman who'd just met an old friend of mine and knew nothing of her situation. My friend started to weep with sheer relief at this unexpected naming of truth: God's transforming grace was touching her very profoundly.

What a lot of naming and renaming in today's verses! When John the Baptist names his cousin 'Lamb of God', what do John's disciples understand by the phrase? They're attracted but call Jesus simply 'Rabbi' (Teacher). Yet, after Jesus invites them along for the day, Andrew goes to tell his brother Simon that they've found the Christ/Messiah/Anointed One. Straight away Jesus renames Simon (meaning 'to hear intelligently') as 'Stone' or 'Rock'—an unlikely identity for this impetuous fisherman. Yet, later, to Jesus' question, 'Who do you say that I am?' Simon Peter proves himself by answering, 'You are the Christ, the Son of the living God.' Jesus replies, 'Blessed are you, Simon son of Jonah, for this was not revealed to you by man, but by my Father in heaven. And I tell you that you are Peter, and on this rock I will build my church' (Matthew 16:15–18).

On first seeing Nathanael, Jesus names him 'a true Israelite, in whom there is nothing false.' Nathanael declares, 'Rabbi, you are the Son of God; you are the King of Israel' (vv. 47, 49). Which comes first? Our naming him in a moment of revelation, or his (re-)naming us? Perhaps the two run in parallel. As we know more of his true name and nature, he calls into being ours—the name and nature that, though dented by life, are what he always intended for us.

....

Lord, any one name reveals only a small part of you. Show me more of yourself, so I can better act and live in your name and be what you named me to be for you.

CL

The grace to rename

'Teacher, this woman was caught in the act of adultery. In the Law Moses commanded us to stone such women. Now what do you say?' … 'Neither do I condemn you,' Jesus declared. 'Go now and leave your life of sin.'

Why do we put name-labels on people? Good, bad, foreign, Roman Catholic, Pentecostal, riff-raff, snob, blind, tart, past-it, badly behaved, unclean, not my kind of person…? It makes decisions easier, or seems to; it stops us getting hurt and causing offence.

Jesus wasn't good at name-labels. Welcoming noisy children, ignoring labels like 'Samaritan', 'loose woman' and 'unclean', he healed the child of a hated Roman officer and called out the name of a cheating tax collector, inviting himself to tea. Thus he caused much offence among certain people and did get hurt, even killed. But, in putting his love for others above defending his own life, he turned bad names and characters into good.

'Filthy whore!' 'Deserves-to-die!' Name-calling can precede violence, but Jesus' presence gave 'Adulterer' the opportunity to leave her life of sin. I wonder if some of those combative religious leaders, acknowledging that they weren't guiltless, repented too. We don't know—but labelling others as different and inferior is unlikely to change them. Only Jesus' grace can do that. In today's story he didn't know the woman's name: presumably the religious leaders hadn't allowed her that dignity, calling her only 'Adulteress'. Although it's clear that she has sinned, Jesus renames her 'Woman'.

I read an article once in *TearFund Times*. Certain Indian women had been expelled from their homes and left destitute for no fault of their own: I think they'd produced only female babies. Christians were befriending them, helping them and their daughters to find shelter, food, work, dignity—renaming them 'Women'.

....

Spend some time asking God about the name-labels you use for different people. How might you change things for someone who bears a derogatory name in your community?

CL

Name-calling

As [Elisha] was walking along the road, some youths came out of the town and jeered at him. 'Go on up, you baldhead!' they said. 'Go on up, you baldhead!' He turned around, looked at them and called down a curse on them in the name of the Lord.

What a strange story! Straight away two bears come out of the woods and maul 42 of the youths. Most commentaries struggle to justify it. Surely this mighty prophet should have been able to rise above being called 'baldy' by some ignorant youths—even if he was just at the start of his ministry, probably grieving and possibly insecure?

Elisha's mentor and predecessor, Elijah, had just ascended in a fiery chariot to heaven—and it may have been that the 'Go up' part of the youths' insult touched a sore spot: 'Get up outta here, like Elijah is meant to have done!' Bethel, his destination, was a centre for calf-worship, endorsed by bad King Ahab, so maybe God was being insulted along with his new wonder-prophet.

We live under a new 'contract'. Early Christians were called cannibals because they 'ate the flesh and drank the blood' of Jesus, but they didn't curse their persecutors. The new covenant's lack of God-sent 'bears' and thunderbolts may be because we are not to curse people. We're to 'turn the other cheek', even to physical violence, as Jesus did.

I don't understand Elisha's cursing but I do know that God doesn't like any of his people being called names, insulted or intimidated. A group of more than 42 taunting youths can be mighty intimidating—but so can a group of respectable middle-class adults when they start insulting youths because they perceive, wrongly, that all young people are violent and of evil intent. I'm sure we all have names far worse than 'baldy' for politicians we despise—I'm afraid I do! But God doesn't want us to despise them, naming them as subhuman, however much we disagree with their policies and actions.

....

Ask God to show you how you can cope better with insults and intimidation. Ask him to show you where you degrade and intimidate others through name-calling.

CL

Renaming as blessing

Jacob was left alone; and a man wrestled with him until daybreak… Jacob said, 'I will not let you go, unless you bless me.' … Then the man said, 'You shall no longer be called Jacob, but Israel, for you have striven with God and with humans, and have prevailed.'

Ever been desperate? It's bad enough when fate seems to be conspiring against us, isn't it? But when we ourselves have been the cause of everything collapsing around us—when, for example, a messed-up relationship is our fault—then we're *really* desperate. Even if, by some miracle, disaster doesn't follow, how can we live with ourselves? And if disaster does follow, we have absolutely nothing—except God.

Jacob's cheating of his brother Esau was coming home to roost. On a journey with his wives, children and everything they possessed, Jacob heard that his brother was coming to find him—with 400 men. Having sent his loved ones across a ford, hoping that they wouldn't suffer what was coming to him, he spent the night alone, wrestling with a 'man' who turned out to be God.

Being left with nothing except God puts us in a good place—so long as, having sunk to the depths of our own despair, we're prepared to repent and lean on him. The second-born of twins, Jacob had tricked his brother out of his birthright as the elder son. He had grasped Esau's heel at birth, and now the wrestling 'man' touches Jacob's hip, putting it out of joint. No longer whole, Jacob walks with a limp but has a new name Israel. The Living Bible translates it as 'one who has power with God'. He'll become a nation, not by his own strength, cleverness or machinations but by leaning on God's power—what a crutch! God has changed Jacob's name and very nature, and will heal the relationship with Esau. One good by-product of disasters can be humility—not to humiliate us but so that we're blessed, as Jacob, his family and nation were blessed.

....

Amid disaster, has God ever helped you to change your very nature—and in the end brought blessing? Do you need to press through now in seeking him?

CL

Communities renamed for his glory

This city shall be to me a name of joy, a praise and a glory before all the nations of the earth who shall hear of all the good that I do for them; they shall fear and tremble because of all the good and all the prosperity I provide.

What a mess: we're told our children's children may still be dealing with it when they grow up! As I write, we're in the worst worldwide recession anyone can remember and it's all our fault. All the richer countries have been living off the poor. Our 'new clothes', which we thought fit for an emperor, have been spun from a great bubble of debt that's burst now. We ourselves may not have cheated and lied but we've benefited from years of seeming prosperity—and now we too are fallen, with many made redundant. Power in the world is shifting; the West is unlikely to remain at its centre and it may well be that those who do move into that position are less benign— towards Christians, if no one else.

This is a great chapter to read in such a situation. Jeremiah 33:3 is known as 'God's telephone number': 'Call to me and I will answer you, and will tell you great and hidden things which you have not known'. Those things were told to Jeremiah, in exile and 'still shut up in the court of the guard' (v. 1). He was there as a good prophet of God, sharing the punishment of his people for their repeated rebellion against God.

Thank God he's concerned not only with the sins of individuals but also with corporate and national sin. Israel's punishment was meant not for retribution but so that they would become for God 'a name of joy, a praise and a glory before all the nations'. He intended not only to forgive and cleanse but to restore and bless them.

Can God's creative grace now imagine London, Sydney, New York or Jerusalem being 'a name of joy, a praise and a glory' for himself?

....

Lord, as people groups straying far from your ways, we need your cleansing, forgiveness and redemption. Give us grace to imagine and then pray and work so that nations' names will bring you joy and praise.

CL

Name and reputation

No longer will they call you Deserted, or name your land Desolate. But you will be called Hephzibah, and your land Beulah; for the Lord will take delight in you, and your land will be married… They will be called the Holy People, the Redeemed of the Lord… Sought After, the City No Longer Deserted.

What an emotive passage, especially for women. The pain of divorce or separation sharpens with the name 'Deserted'. Even if people aren't thinking, 'Her husband's left her—there must be a good reason!' it's easy to believe that they are. There are names, too, for the never-married: Frustrated Spinster, Bitter Old Maid, Left On The Shelf or, biggest 'sin' of all in the present age, 'Sexually Repressed'.

Do you know people who are 'Desolate'? These days we might call them 'Depressed'. The feared name-label 'clinical depression' describes something so swiftly increasing, especially among young people, that soon it will be second only to heart disease as the most disabling condition worldwide.

Today's Bible passage refers to a whole nation with rock-bottom prospects and reputation, yet God was saying that he would call them 'Hephzibah' (which means 'my delight is in her') and 'Beulah' ('married'); 'Holy', 'Redeemed' and 'Sought After'.

God neither sees nor names any of his people as 'Deserted', 'Single' or 'Desolate' but as 'Transformed'. He says, 'The nations will see your righteousness, and all kings your glory; you will be called by a new name that the mouth of the Lord will bestow… a crown of splendour in the Lord's hand, a royal diadem in the hand of your God' (vv. 2–3). We may be divorced, single, clinically depressed or desolate, but he is our Saviour: he sees our 'splendour' as enhancing his own. This is what he's all about—not condemnation but transformation, not calling us names but renaming us.

Meditate on Isaiah 62:1: 'For Jerusalem's sake I will not remain quiet, till her righteousness shines out like the dawn, her salvation like a blazing torch.'

CL

Baptised into Jesus' name

They were baptised into the name of the Lord Jesus… No one can say that you were baptised into my [Paul's] name… You are in Christ Jesus, who has become for us wisdom from God—that is, our righteousness, holiness and redemption.

I can't remember if I was baptised 'in the name of Jesus'; it might have been the Trinity. We'll avoid examining specific rituals or wordings for baptism—God's not a picky bureaucrat—but what does being 'baptised into the name of Jesus' mean? In Acts 19, Paul found some Ephesian believers who'd received John's baptism of repentance, which signalled leaving behind their sin. That prepared the way for Christ, but the full deal involved far more.

'Baptised' simply means 'submersed'. If you leave a pan soaking in a bowlful of water, it's 'baptised': the water is inside, outside and all around it. Substitute 'pan' for 'me' and 'water' for 'Jesus'—that's how we're to live. Being submersed in him leaves no room for sin.

Why 'into his name'? 1 Corinthians 1 shows us how that makes Christian baptism specific. No one—Peter, Paul, Apollos, whoever—can start a new religion in their own name. It's all about Jesus Christ. Whatever baptism's precise wording and ritual, with Jesus at the centre we're all one in him, as he is one with the Father and Holy Spirit. (Note how the Holy Spirit loves joining in the Jesus-submersion.)

But why his *name*? 'Jesus' means 'one who saves people from their sins' (Matthew 1:21). Despite our repentance, we lack power to live sinlessly without continual submersion in Saviour Jesus. 'Christ' means 'anointed, chosen'. He invites us to live soaked in his nature—his wisdom, righteousness, holiness and redemption, his humility, suffering, resurrection, truth, joy, love and life. Of ourselves we may not be wise or influential (1 Corinthians 1:26) but we're baptised into and live submersed in the name of Jesus, the name above all names.

Know his cleansing, soothing, refreshing water removing all the grime and stress of the day. It's better than a flotation tank!

CL

Called by God's name!

'Fear not, for I have redeemed you; I have summoned you by name; you are mine… Bring my sons from afar and my daughters from the ends of the earth—everyone who is called by my name, whom I created for my glory, whom I formed and made.'

When I worked part-time in a lowly administrative role, I'd sign certain correspondence 'pp', which means 'per pro' or 'as from' an appropriate person in authority. That's the same principle as praying in Jesus name: 'If two of you on earth agree about anything you ask for, it will be done for you by my Father in heaven. For where two or three come together in my name, there am I with them' (Matthew 18:19–20).

We may be puny on our own but we have Jesus' authority in all kinds of situations. As Isaiah 43:2 says, 'When you pass through the waters, I will be with you; and when you pass through the rivers, they will not sweep over you. When you walk through the fire, you will not be burned; the flames will not set you ablaze.' We shouldn't test that out with actual fires or rivers, but I'm sure we've all experienced God's presence with us in places that are dangerous for our mind, body and/or spirit. He helps us pass safely through to the other side when we'd have gone under on our own.

We are each individually called by our own name to be his—and, as if that wasn't enough, we are then called by and known by his name, to be his glory. If a child's dad is the police chief and she's known by his name, no one's going to mess with her! But if the police chief considers his daughter his glory, precious and honoured in his sight—well…!

Isaiah's prophecy came to a people who had been punished by God, exiled, left behind and scattered, but still they are called by God's name, to be his glory.

....

Pray for your biological or Spirit-birthed children who are not in a good situation: 'Bring my sons from afar and my daughters from the ends of the earth.'

CL

Named in the book of life

My co-workers, whose names are in the book of life… 'To everyone who conquers I will give… a white stone, and on the white stone is written a new name that no one knows except the one who receives it… I will write on you the name of my God, and the name of the city of my God… and my own new name.'

Why are lists of names recorded for posterity? Because they're considered important to remember for some special reason. They may appear on war memorials, in books of remembrance or on wall-mounted lists of past office-holders—mayors in a town hall or vicars in a church.

There's much important name-recording in the last pages of the New Testament—on books, stones, even people. There are old and new names, familiar and mysterious ones, names of individual people, of a city and of God. Presumably they're recorded for our benefit, since God won't forget even billions of our names, or his own names!

I had thought the recording of names all happened in the book of Revelation, but Paul mentions the 'book of life' as he pleads with his fellow workers in Philippi to help two women in dispute with each other. According to Revelation 2, 'book of life' names are of those who have 'conquered' or 'overcome'. Euodia and Syntyche need to overcome their quarrel, their warring attitude, and Paul asks their fellow Christians to help them. We too can look out for one another.

In Revelation, the fact that God records these 'life' names could be an encouragement in the face of the Roman state's 'death' lists, but I sense there's far more that I don't understand. We are being given a glimpse of a new heaven and a new earth and life's unimaginable richness beyond death. Being given a white stone and a new name is exciting, but God's name written on us is far better! Is that why we won't even want to sin? And what will his new name be? We are allowed to dream, to imagine, to be encouraged.

....

'See, I have given you authority… over all the power of the enemy… Nevertheless, do not rejoice at this… but rejoice that your names are written in heaven' (Luke 10:20).

CL

Now that we have considered the importance of names in the Bible, Ali Herbert helps us to focus on the names of God.

When we are introduced to someone, invariably the first thing we are told about them is their name. People's names are integral to identifying them: frankly, if you're known as a number, it's never good. Once we've known someone well, we even tend to ascribe their characteristics, both good and bad, to others with the same name. If we bump into an acquaintance and don't remember what they're called, it's pretty embarrassing and we flounder in the conversation. A name is important to us.

In the Old Testament we have a somewhat peculiar introduction to God. The names 'Elohim', meaning 'god' or 'gods', and 'Yahweh' appear fairly early on (translated as 'God' and 'the LORD God' in Genesis 2), but it's not until the book of Exodus, when Moses has a frightening experience with a burning bush, that things begin to get (only a little) clearer. Moses questions the powerful being who is speaking from the bush about his identity, and the final answer is not entirely satisfying: it is 'I AM who I AM'. Well, thanks very much, that's really helpful!

Scholars have argued over the years what this name could mean. Is God implying that he is the very essence of everything, that he is so big that his very existence is an answer in itself? Those are probably deep questions to ponder when you next have a quiet decade or two—so instead, for the next couple of weeks, we're going to look at some of the names that God is called (and calls himself) as he begins to reveal a little more over the generations. These names are like spots of colour dripped on a canvas, which gradually build up and merge to create the masterpiece, the true nature of our amazing God—loving and just and gracious and awesome and wild. There are lots of indications of the wonderful character of God in his many different names, so it's a great opportunity to get to know him a little better.

El-Shaddai: Almighty God

When Abram was ninety-nine years old, the Lord appeared to him and said, 'I am God Almighty; walk before me and be blameless. I will confirm my covenant between me and you and will greatly increase your numbers.'

Have you ever had a 'mountaintop' experience of meeting with God? Maybe in an awesome cathedral, at a Christian conference or during a special time of worship? After an experience like that, we often feel we could do anything for him, that we could live blameless lives, our focus, energy and passion poured out for God's will and his purpose. That feeling may last days or it may last minutes. We are ordinary human beings, wanting to follow God but blown this way and that by the winds of everyday life.

If we had an experience like Abram's, would we manage to press on a little longer in God's will? I don't know. We are called to be blameless, which certainly seems impossible, but God doesn't leave us alone to struggle on and feel like failures. Of course we all fall down on our Christian walk, of course we all turn in circles and feel we can't carry on, but God is nothing like us (thank God). He is almighty, always. He is powerful and perfect—and, what is more, he offers us some of that strength and power for whatever circumstance we face today.

God has a plan and a purpose for you. Abram was old and without children, yet God made extravagant promises to him. We believe in the same God today, who makes extravagant promises to us and keeps them. He is almighty—there is no need for him to promise us anything, and yet he does. Let's praise him today that not only is he way above any other power, but that he comes as close to us as a breath, to give us the strength we need to get through the day.

....

Look at the sky or the stars and consider that our Almighty God created them. Then consider that the same God breathes his strength into you today... as much as you will need.

AH

Adonai: Lord and Master

[Abram] said, 'If I have found favour in your eyes, my lord, do not pass your servant by. Let a little water be brought, and then you may all wash your feet and rest under this tree. Let me get you something to eat, so you can be refreshed and then go on your way.'

Who is the most important person you have ever entertained in your home? A celebrity? An overseas visitor? A much-loved family member? I bet you pulled out all the stops, got the best crockery out and served your most delicious food—and plenty of it. In this passage, Abraham welcomes his visitors with open arms, offering hospitality at its best. Somehow he knows that these visitors are a little out of the ordinary and is happy to call himself 'your servant'. His acts of service are to be rewarded with a shocking statement—that Sarah, his elderly wife, will give him a child within the year (v. 10).

The word for 'lord' used in this passage is 'Adonai'. To God's people, the name 'Yahweh' was so holy that it couldn't be said out loud, so instead they used 'Adonai'. This was a common term meaning 'master' or 'lord'—and we get a sense of that meaning in Abraham's deference to his special guests. Over the last few decades we've learnt (from writers like Adrian Plass) that 'God is nice and he likes me'. This is incredibly important for us to understand, but sometimes we can fall into the opposite trap of thinking that God is no more powerful than a well-worn teddy bear. With the name Adonai, we are reminded that he is totally in authority above us, as our master and lord.

This knowledge compels us to submit our lives to him and, like Abraham, to recognise the privilege of being a servant and worshipper of this God. Don't we sometimes get it upside down—acting as if God is there to serve us? Of course he utterly loves us and knows the best for us in every way, but our job is to serve him, to find out what pleases him, to enjoy him and worship him.

....

Read Philippians 2:5–11 to see how Jesus took the role of servant to the extreme. Then use these verses to inspire you as you praise him.

AH

El-Olam: Everlasting God

Abraham planted a tamarisk tree in Beersheba, and there he called upon the name of the Lord, the Eternal God.

Abraham is meeting once again with Abimelech, the Philistine leader, with whom he has previously made a treaty. The Philistines were a powerful tribe but Abimelech is clearly anxious that Abraham and his God will prove dangerous, saying, 'God is with you in everything you do…' (v. 22). Abimelech has brought his chief military commander with him to broker a deal—a sign of escalating threat. But the tension is defused as Abraham carefully agrees a peace deal and clears up confusion over a seized well, which would have been a vital commodity in the desert region where they lived. As a result of these delicate negotiations, verse 34 tells us that 'Abraham stayed in the land of the Philistines for a long time'.

Abraham recognises that he has been blessed and made secure, and praises the 'Eternal God', a God who has no beginning and no end. My daughter Gracie is nearly five and has become somewhat obsessed with the concept of infinity. She has recently learnt to count 'all the way to a hundred!'—although, if you ask her about a hundred and one, she will screw up her face and look concerned. One of her teachers has mentioned the idea of infinity to her and she really wants to know what it means. Is it a number you can count to? Why not? What is bigger than infinity?

Well, I'm no mathematician but I do know that infinity is beyond my imagination. This is the wonderful idea that Abraham is ascribing to God—the concept that God is beyond time and space, truly beyond our imagination. As Revelation 4:8 puts it, God 'was, and is, and is to come'. He is everlasting, eternal and infinite, clearly seeing the past, present and future. Who wouldn't want a God like that on their side?

....

Lord God, you see me from your heavenly, infinite perspective; you see my life laid out before you. Thank you that you are beyond my imagining. Strengthen me for this journey.

AH

Jehovah Jireh: the Lord my Provider

[Abraham] went over and took the ram and sacrificed it as a burnt offering instead of his son. So Abraham called that place The Lord Will Provide. And to this day it is said, 'On the mountain of the Lord it will be provided.'

Goodness me, this story is traumatic! This is the stuff of nightmares. While human sacrifice was not unheard of in Abraham's culture, Isaac had been a miraculous answer to God's promise. Surely a loving God wouldn't demand him back like this? Nonetheless, Abraham hears God's voice clearly and obeys him immediately, and God the Provider transforms the situation.

Part of the meaning of 'Jehovah Jireh' is that God 'sees', and it's wonderful to know that God sees our need before we even know about it. Then, as part of his very nature, he provides the perfect solution. When my husband Nick and I were engaged, we had very little money to pay for a honeymoon. A few weeks before the wedding we were handed an anonymous envelope with £500 in cash inside: our honeymoon was provided for. We didn't have anywhere to live either (I know, we don't sound very organised!) but, just three weeks before the wedding, some friends told us they were going travelling and that we could stay in their lovely house: our home was provided for.

I could tell you so many examples of God providing physically, spiritually, mentally and emotionally for me over the years—a word to lift me out of depression, a sorely needed phone call, work, peace in a stressful situation and so on. There have been answers to prayer in their thousands; I'm sure you could tell me the same. God doesn't always provide in the way we expect, and often not until the last minute. This is not to be mean but to teach us to listen and obey and trust. It's the most important thing we can do. His name is God the Provider: let's trust that he does just that.

....

Ask God for something specific today, for something that has been on your heart—and look for his answer.

AH

Jehovah Rophe: the Lord my Healer

'If you listen carefully to the voice of the Lord your God and do what is right in his eyes, if you pay attention to his commands and keep all his decrees, I will not bring on you any of the diseases I brought on the Egyptians, for I am the Lord, who heals you.'

A young woman has a devastating car crash, leaving her unable to walk or talk properly. You pray for her: a year later she walks down the aisle to be married and is renowned for giving great talks. A friend has suspected cancer. You pray for her, and the doctors scan further and say it is just previously unnoticed scar tissue. A child has a serious accident. You pray and he recovers far more quickly than the doctors expected. These are all real situations. Are they coincidences or does God really live up to his name as the Healer?

Obviously the subject of healing is very painful for many of us, as we know that not everyone we pray for does have a miraculous story of healing. But God by his nature longs to bring healing and wholeness to us, and while he clearly did so for people in the Bible and early Church, he hasn't stopped today. Unexpected healing was as surprising to the people of the Bible as it is to us now, yet it seems easier to believe in healings we read about than those in our own lives.

True as ever to the character of God, Jesus said that he had come to do three things—heal the sick, cast out demons and set the captives free—and he told his disciples (which includes us) to do the same. Of course we want everyone to be healed, and we also know that, this side of heaven, it simply isn't going to happen. John Wimber of the Vineyard movement prayed for sick people every week for a year before anything happened at all. Then all heaven broke loose and many people were healed. But if just one person is made better in their body, mind or spirit, isn't it worth praying time and time again?

....

Healing is not about us or how 'good' we are; it's about God longing to bring wholeness to us. Pray for someone you know who is sick today.

AH

Jehovah Nissi: the Lord my Banner

Then the Lord said to Moses, 'Write this on a scroll as something to be remembered and make sure that Joshua hears it, because I will completely blot out the memory of Amalek from under heaven.' Moses built an altar and called it The Lord is my Banner.

It may be that your church is the sort that has wonderful, creative banners inside, with images of doves and rainbows and swirling colours that help you focus on God as you worship. It may be that your church has banners outside, with a slightly different tone, saying things such as, 'How will you spend eternity—Smoking or Non-Smoking?' and, 'If you think it's hot here, imagine hell'. I'm not entirely sure how the second variety imagine they are reaching out to people, although maybe (I hope) they are tongue-in-cheek.

The type of banner that Moses had in mind when he called God by this name was slightly different from our kind. It was a banner like a medieval 'standard' or flag that fluttered on a pole at the head of an army. This banner wasn't simply for decoration but served three significant purposes: to show everyone exactly who the army belonged to, to be a point of rally in the midst of battle and to create an area where the soldiers could receive new orders in the chaos. While your banner was flying high, you were still in the fight.

This is a fantastic visual image of God as a focal point for our church, a place where we can run when we're afraid, where we can receive our orders and where we can stand to show that we belong to Jesus Christ. Make no mistake, in our current climate as Christians we are in a battle. That is becoming more and more clear as the moral, political and religious landscape shifts. It is going to be of vital importance to know who we are standing with, how we can hear God's voice to receive our orders, where our safety lies and just who we are fighting for.

....

Lord, we pray for our country. We pray that once again your name will be honoured and lifted up. Give us the strength we need for all that lies ahead. Amen

AH

Jehovah T'sabaoth: the Lord of Hosts

This is what the Lord Almighty says: 'Administer true justice; show mercy and compassion to one another. Do not oppress the widow or the fatherless, the alien or the poor. In your hearts do not think evil of each other.'

My husband Nick and I enjoy watching TV programmes such as *Britain's Got Talent* and *The X Factor*, but I think that these and many other 'reality' shows tell us a lot about our society's values. Many of these programmes are obsessed with taking an obscure, non-rich person and making them an instant rich celebrity hit, with or without talent. The message is that power comes to the rich and famous and, more importantly, that meaning and joy can be found with them, too.

In our passage today, the NIV translates this name of God as 'Lord Almighty' but a better translation is 'Lord of Hosts'. 'Hosts' can be three things—armies, angels or stars—and, like the name we looked at yesterday, the word carries overtones of battle. So within this name for God is the concept of his incredible power and authority: God 'The Supreme Captain of the Angels'; God 'In Authority Over Every Earthly Army'; God 'Ruler of the Billions of Galaxies'. Wow! But what do we see here of this immensely powerful God? Is he communing with kings, rearranging a universe or sending angels to do his bidding? No. Although God has ultimate power, his entire focus here is on the widow, the orphan, the refugee, the poor and dispossessed.

Again we see the incredible paradox of the Creator of the universe coming close, caring deeply for the intimate details of people's lives, for the lost, the last and the least. At the core of our faith is the awesome Lord God of Hosts, whose remit is nothing to do with celebrity and wealth but instead is about justice, mercy and compassion. It is a challenge for us as we reflect on our attitude to the people who surround us.

....

Have a look at Jesus' words of blessing in Luke 6:20–22. Pray for people in those situations and see if you can help someone in a specific and practical way today.

AH

Jehovah Magen: the Lord my Shield

As for God, his way is perfect; the word of the Lord is flawless. He is a shield for all who take refuge in him. For who is God besides the Lord? And who is the Rock except our God? It is God who arms me with strength and makes my way perfect.

Are you up against it right now? Do you have to deal with difficult circumstances on a daily basis? Perhaps you're coping with the stress of work or not working, relationships that are not straightforward, your body not behaving the way it should? Well, there is some good news. God introduces himself as a shield to Abram in Genesis 15:1 and says to him, 'Do not be afraid.' As this psalm shows us, a shield does not guarantee that there won't be a struggle but it does offer active protection in the middle of it. You don't need a shield if you're not in a war. It's of no earthly use if you're just hanging out by the swimming pool. This is one piece of equipment designed for getting out there, for being dangerous, despite being under attack.

Corrie Ten Boom, a Dutch survivor of Ravensbruck concentration camp during World War II, tells the story (in *The Hiding Place*, Hodder & Stoughton, 1971) of being desperate to take her Bible into the dreaded camp under the eyes of the ruthless guards. As the queue of frightened women moved along, guards twice searched every person, including the woman in front of her and the woman behind her, but completely ignored Corrie. That Bible was a lifeline to her and many others in a dark place over the coming months and years. God was true to his nature and shielded her in a very physical sense.

The apostle Paul, in Ephesians 6:16, talks of taking up the 'shield of faith' to put out the flaming arrows of the evil one. We believe that we are not only protected by the shield, but that as we take up the 'sword of the Spirit' (v. 17) with our free hand, we are also able to do some damage in this spiritual battle.

....

Ask God to be your shield today.

AH

Jehovah Misgabbi: the Lord my High Tower

Whoever dwells in the shelter of the Most High will rest in the shadow of the Almighty. I will say of the Lord, 'He is my refuge and my fortress, my God, in whom I trust.'... A thousand may fall at your side, ten thousand at your right hand, but it will not come near you.

I love this psalm. It speaks of the total security and safety of trusting God as he offers us his protection, his deliverance, his salvation, his answer, his rescue, his refuge, his faithfulness, his shelter and his rest. What a list! Those are things I need day in, day out, not just for the big issues of life but as I struggle to get my kids to school, fight with shopping bags, try to juggle finances, answer telephone calls, cry with friends going through hard times, read the day's new troubles in the newspapers and so on.

Unlike the picture of the shield, which is designed for action, the idea of God as my 'high tower' or my fortress brings a sense of relief: I know I can be safe and rest for a while within thick, impenetrable walls. From the walls of a tower, things can look quite different, too. We gain a 'bird's eye view' and a new perspective on the lie of the land. We can check that our boundaries are guarded well and can thank God for the good things we see he has provided for us. What's more, from the walls of a safe, high tower, the enemy looks small, insignificant and considerably less dangerous. He can't even get to us!

There are many times when we want to retreat from a situation. God the High Tower knows that and has already prepared a place we can go to when we feel tired, confused and scared. In verse 15 God says, 'You will call upon me, and I will answer you; I will be with you in trouble, I will deliver you and honour you.'

....

Take a few minutes to rest in the safety of the High Tower. Ask the Holy Spirit to refresh you and restore you as you go on in the day.

AH

Jehovah Go'el: the Lord my Redeemer

'You will forget the shame of your youth and remember no more the reproach of your widowhood. For your Maker is your husband—the Lord Almighty is his name—the Holy One of Israel is your Redeemer; he is called the God of all the earth.'

Do you enjoy shopping? If so, I expect you love snapping up a bargain at the sales. As we look at this name for God, we may wonder if God has got it the wrong way round. He paid an enormous price for something that he could have considered quite worthless.

In the Old Testament, a 'redeemer' was a person who either bought back a piece of land or a slave or paid off someone's debt. Alternatively, when a woman had been widowed, her husband's brother could marry her to save her from poverty, and he was known as a 'kinsman redeemer'. In the book of Ruth we hear the story of a widow looking after her mother-in-law Naomi and eventually being saved by a 'kinsman redeemer' named Boaz, who steps in to save the day. Isaiah 54 shows us a picture of God himself in this role, stepping in to save and restore his people who have been abandoned.

If you have a dramatic conversion story, you'll be fully aware of what the Lord has 'redeemed' you from. Even those of us who don't have such a story will know of endless ways in which God continues to rescue us and forgive us. Jesus, of course, is the fulfilment of the promise of redemption as he finally pays the full price for our rebellion against God. So I am redeemed, fully paid-off and ready to go—but I still do things wrong. I keep acting as though I'm owned by someone else, even though I don't mean to. I think that's called 'sin'—so I'm grateful the Lord continues to redeem me day by day.

We also believe that we have a purpose once we are redeemed, which is to worship God in spirit and truth, and let other people know about this one-off, endless, eternal offer.

....

If my kinsman-redeemer is a king, what does that make me?

AH

Jehovah Rohi: the Lord my Shepherd

The Lord is my shepherd, I shall not be in want. He makes me lie down in green pastures, he leads me beside quiet waters, he restores my soul… Surely goodness and love will follow me all the days of my life, and I will dwell in the house of the Lord for ever.

For a time after I gave birth to my first child, I felt quite cut off from church and from any spiritual inspiration. Then I decided to use the final breast-feed of the evening to try to pray, as the baby was peaceful and settled before her sleep. I learnt the words of Psalm 23 and said them out loud each evening for about a year. Every evening, I found something different to focus on, something different that I felt God was pointing out to me. It was a special time.

This is such a famous psalm but an analogy using sheep is not the easiest for us to get our minds around today. However, sheep were everywhere in the world of the Bible. To speak of God as a shepherd would have been like describing him as the driver of your car or the big boss of your company. David was simply speaking from his own life experience as a young man. He knew what a shepherd had to do—how a shepherd cared for his sheep at the risk of his own life, how he made sure they were fed and watered and safe. He also knew that it was a seriously low-status job, dirty, dangerous and often boring. Yet we see that God is prepared to take this job on for us in the person of Jesus, who later describes himself as the good shepherd.

In John 10, Jesus talks at length along these lines, about the sheep knowing their shepherd, listening to his voice and following him—and about the shepherd being prepared to die for his flock. The significance of his use of this special name was not missed by his audience, who clearly knew that he was claiming to be God. From this time on, Jesus was a marked man.

....

Thank Jesus for his love and care. He is the good shepherd, the one who knows you better than you know yourself.

Read John 10 to see Jesus taking on and explaining this name for God in his own words.

AH

Jehovah Shalom: the Lord is Peace

But the Lord said to him, 'Peace! Do not be afraid. You are not going to die.' So Gideon built an altar to the Lord there and called it The Lord is Peace.

Is there anyone who wouldn't like more peace in their life? You might want physical peace, if you live in a noisy city, or perhaps mental peace, if you are anxious about a particular situation. It seems to be the one thing that our world agrees on: peace is a good thing. Yet, while most of us appear to be on a permanent search for it, it seems to be a rather elusive state. Money can't buy it, genius doesn't guarantee it, beauty won't lead you to it and celebrity seems to be the antithesis of it.

The search for peace, and the peddling of a poor reflection of it, is big business, but true peace isn't just the absence of violence or a vague sense of tranquillity. The meaning behind this name for God is much fuller than that. The Hebrew word *shalom* denotes wholeness and a sense of being complete. This peace is possible even when there is a 'sea of troubles', as Shakespeare put it (*Hamlet*).

In today's Bible passage, Gideon is seriously scared of the Midianites and is threshing wheat, rather bizarrely, in a winepress. This was an interesting choice as the threshing process needs wind to work, and a winepress is not a natural wind-trap. However, the Lord greets this frightened young man rather optimistically as 'mighty warrior' and calls him to save Israel. Gideon's terror at realising that he has encountered the living God is not necessarily a bad reaction—but the Lord's immediate word to him is, 'Peace!' Gideon will need that wholeness and quiet confidence in God if he is to be an effective soldier and leader in all that is to come.

As Christians, we have the answer to our world's ongoing search for peace. It is even our God's name.

....

'And the peace of God, which transcends all understanding, will guard your hearts and your minds in Christ Jesus' (Philippians 4:7).

AH

Jesus: Son of the Most High

But the angel said to her, 'Do not be afraid, Mary, you have found favour with God. You will be with child and give birth to a son, and you are to give him the name Jesus. He will be great and will be called the Son of the Most High.'

This is startling and amazing news! Mary and her ancestors have worshipped the 'Most High' for generations, leading back through history to Abraham; and now, at a particular moment in time, the Most High is causing a child to be born to this young Jewish girl. The Son of God is about to enter our broken and hurting world. It's a wonderful image of the Trinity, the three persons of God—the Father and the Holy Spirit, who will 'overshadow' Mary, working together to create Jesus, the Son.

This is the crux of our faith. Is Jesus really the Son of God? Most people—and all serious historians—will acknowledge that Jesus was a real person who lived and died 2000 years ago in the Middle East. Many people believe he was a prophet or teacher, but from that point onwards, many accept a caricature of our faith and never look deeper into the claims that this man was truly the Son of God. Jesus certainly believed he was God's one and only Son. The disciples believed it, too, as most of them went to their grisly deaths defending that very fact. The early Church believed it, as its members were persecuted and hid in catacombs to worship him. Do you?

If Jesus is the Son of the Most High, not only must we worship him as God but we should also remember that we too are adopted sons and daughters of that same God. As Jesus himself says in Luke 6:35, 'Love your enemies, do good to them, and lend to them without expecting to get anything back. Then your reward will be great, and you will be children of the Most High.'

....

Meditate on 1 John 3:23, which says, 'And this is his command: to believe in the name of his Son, Jesus Christ, and to love one another as he commanded us.'

AH

Jesus: the Messiah

The woman said, 'I know that Messiah' (called Christ) 'is coming. When he comes, he will explain everything to us.' Then Jesus declared, 'I who speak to you am he.'

As our study of God's names draws to a close, it's appropriate to finish with the name of Jesus Christ. Jesus Christ is the fulfilment of all the names of God—Healer, Redeemer and so on. Jesus Christ is the gate (John 10:7) to life for us. Jesus Christ calls us towards him, man and God rolled into one.

We often think of the name 'Christ' as if it is Jesus' surname, but it is actually a Greek translation of the Hebrew word 'Messiah', meaning 'Anointed One'. The Messiah was the promised king for whom the people of God had been waiting for centuries. He would come and finally set the Israelites free from all oppression, giving them military victory over all other peoples. They were expecting someone a little like King David but perhaps more powerful, so, when Jesus arrived on the scene with a ragtag bunch of followers, from an insignificant town, riding on a common donkey and finally being executed by the Romans, people were quick to dismiss him for not living up to their long-held expectations. That is, until some looked a little closer and realised that Jesus perfectly fulfilled everything the prophets had promised, from where he was born to how he died. They realised that the oppression they were freed from was not just another military threat but, rather, the ultimate enemy—death.

Of course, the disciples didn't need this intellectual argument to know that Jesus was in fact the Messiah, and neither did the Samaritan woman at the well in today's reading. They had encountered him for themselves and heard his claims. Their lives were transformed completely. This is the incredible God we worship.

....

Spend some time thanking and worshipping Jesus for all he is: Master, Almighty God, Strength-giver, Everlasting, Provider, Healer, Banner, Lord of Hosts, Shield, High Tower, Redeemer, Shepherd, Peace, Most High, Messiah.

AH

▶ ▶ PRAYER FOCUS

We've spent nearly a month looking at the biblical theme of names and naming—the names we give ourselves and others, and the many names by which God can be known.

On 2 July, Chris Leonard wrote, 'As we know more of his true name and nature, he calls into being ours—the name and nature that, though dented by life, are what he always intended for us.'

Look back at the names of God that Ali Herbert has been explaining over the last two weeks. Did one of these names seem especially meaningful to you? Settle yourself in quietness before God and meditate on that name, asking yourself the question, 'If God is this, what does that make me?' (see page 91).

Thank God for the insights he gives you.

'Meet Jeremiah,' says Diana Archer, who will be leading us through the next two weeks of daily readings.

It could be that one of the most often-quoted verses of the Bible was originally uttered by Jeremiah: '"For I know the plans I have for you," declares the Lord, "plans to prosper you and not to harm you, plans to give you hope and a future"' (Jeremiah 29:11). This was probably the only verse I knew from the book of Jeremiah for a long time. I quoted it to others and depended on it myself, but that was all I really knew of Jeremiah, apart from a few vague impressions of a prophet of doom and something to do with a potter. It never occurred to me to find out what that comforting verse was originally all about.

This goes to show how easy it is to miss out on the treasures of God's word, just because we think it might be a bit difficult to read. Despite being a self-confessed fanatic of theological study, somehow I had let Jeremiah slip through the net. I am not proud of this. The only redeeming feature is that suddenly discovering the riches of a part of the Bible you did not know well before is a heady experience. I have become fascinated by the man and his message. I hope that, whether you know Jeremiah far better than I did or whether he is as yet an un-known friend, the next two weeks will prove enlightening.

A bit of background to start with: Jeremiah prophesied in Judah from 626 to 586BC, some of the most tumultuous years in that country and, indeed, in the whole region. Egypt, Assyria and Babylon were the con-temporary superpowers, jostling for supremacy. Judah was caught in the crossfire, first taken over by Egypt and then by Babylon. As a priest, Jeremiah tried to advise the succession of kings of Judah, from Josiah to Zedekiah, and warn them that the consequences of not trusting in God would be the destruction of the nation. Jeremiah ended up in exile in Egypt after an extraordinary life, dominated by the word of God that came to him and the trouble it got him into.

The call

The word of the Lord came to me, saying, 'Before I formed you in the womb I knew you, before you were born I set you apart; I appointed you as a prophet to the nations.' 'Ah, Sovereign Lord,' I said, 'I do not know how to speak; I am only a child.' But the Lord said to me, 'Do not say, "I am only a child."'

This was where it all began for Jeremiah. As a priest, his life would have revolved around the daily rituals and patterns of worship. It was all he knew—he was the son of the priest Hilkiah from Anathoth (v. 1)—but now God singled him out and spoke to him in an unmistakable way. While we don't know exactly how Jeremiah heard the word of the Lord, there was clearly no doubt for him that it was the word of the Lord. From that point on, his life was not his own.

Jeremiah's initial reaction was hesitant: 'I do not know how to speak; I am only a child' (v. 6). Isn't it reassuring how often characters in the Bible—people like Moses, Sarah and Gideon—react with reluctance when God calls them? Jeremiah was clearly not jumping with joy at his summons to be a prophet to the nations, but then it does sound like a rather large task. Perhaps he knew that the prophet's lot was not an easy one. Yet experience suggests that God usually calls us to something outside our natural capabilities and comfort zones. God based his claim on Jeremiah's life on the fact that he had created him, and the same applies to us. Jeremiah was called to a specific task at a specific time, and some Christians have a comparable definite calling to a job, country or vocation, but each of us is called by name (Revelation 3:5) and created for a purpose (Ephesians 2:10). Each of us can depend on God being with us, just as he said to Jeremiah, 'Do not be afraid of them, for I am with you and will rescue you' (v. 8).

....

How aware are you of God's calling on your life, and how would you define it? Listen out for his word to you.

Read John 1:35–51 to compare how Jesus called his disciples with the call of Jeremiah.

DA

The grief

'What fault did your ancestors find in me, that they strayed so far from me? ... They did not ask, "Where is the Lord, who brought us up out of Egypt and led us through the barren wilderness...?"'

From the moment Jeremiah accepted the commission from God to be his spokesman, it seems that the prophet-in-making was catapulted into a maelstrom of passion and pronouncements. Jeremiah's book is not a short one and into it is poured a potent mix of pain, longing, anger and specific prophetic utterance. It is almost as if God was waiting for a channel for his thoughts, and in Jeremiah he found a man through whom his pent-up longing could find expression. It burst forth right from the start as the Lord's frustration with and love for his people were revealed. Right away Jeremiah recorded that there would be judgment on the land of Judah for their 'wickedness in forsaking me' (1:16), threatening national disaster from the land north of the country—presumably Babylon. Yet at the same time, as in the quoted passage above, there is the heartfelt cry of an abandoned lover, desperate because his beloved one has deserted him.

Perhaps it is understandable that Jeremiah hesitated before putting on his prophetic mantle, for this was a difficult message to convey and one that few would want to hear. No one wants to be told either that they have done wrong or that disaster looms. The people of Judah's major sin was defined as a turning away from the God with whom they had a covenant relationship. This was their number one crime. It was so serious that judgment was unavoidable, in accordance with the choice God gave their ancestors many years ago, saying that to choose him was to choose life and to choose any other god was to choose death (Deuteronomy 30:19). Yet punishment is not what God longs for: his heart of love for his people reaches out in the middle even of promises of destruction.

....

How would you define sin?

Read Joshua 24 for some history of the unique relationship between God and his people.

DA

The betrayal

'Be appalled at this, you heavens, and shudder with great horror,' declares the Lord. 'My people have committed two sins: they have forsaken me, the spring of living water, and have dug their own cisterns, broken cisterns that cannot hold water.'

It is incredibly difficult to pick out passages from Jeremiah that are representative of the whole book, because it is so rich, varied and detailed; but this one had to be in here. Jeremiah spelt out the wrong-doing of his compatriots. Judah's turning away from God meant not only that his people had deeply wounded him but also that they had cut themselves off from the source of life. Water was, and is, essential for life, and the imagery here tells us that the substitutes for God to which the people turned could not do the job; they could not supply life.

This seems to me the perfect picture for what we do so easily—shunning the life God holds out to us and preferring instead to go our own way, convinced that we can do it better. Psychologists tell us that, as children, we develop coping strategies for life, which are often flawed, short-term solutions that eventually break down. I know I am not the only one who has had to recognise some of these strategies in my own life and acknowledge that they were, at best, inadequate and, at worst, harmful to myself and those around me. I'm thinking of things like people-pleasing rather than authentic mutual relationships; avoidance rather than honesty and courage, independence rather than the ability to receive. These strategies cause havoc in our worlds and are the opposite of the fullness of life for which God designed us. They are not about living in trust and dependence on God. They are not about enjoying freedom from fear. They are a betrayal of God's love. These are broken cisterns and they are serious. We die if we cannot drink.

....

Dear Father, show me how to turn from my own designs and drink of your living water today and every day. Amen

Read today's passage again, looking at the various ways it refers to water.

DA

The punishment

'A besieging army is coming from a distant land, raising a war cry against the cities of Judah… Your own conduct and actions have brought this upon you. This is your punishment. How bitter it is! How it pierces to the heart!'

Again and again Jeremiah told successive kings that Judah's days were numbered unless the nation returned to true worship of its God. The Judeans had only themselves to blame; they had been warned. The punishment was on its way, yet God's 'fierce anger' (v. 8) was equalled by his pain. This punishment was a last resort. What the Lord longed for was restoration: 'Return, faithless people… for I am your husband. I will choose you' (3:14). So the opposite extremes continue to clash throughout Jeremiah as punishment is threatened and love declared.

These are not easy subjects. It is hard to conceive of God being angry enough to bring destruction, yet tender enough to woo a bride, both at once. Even the ability to identify with that mixture of emotions ourselves—for example, when someone we love hurts us badly—does not help entirely. After all, he is God. Shouldn't he be above those kinds of conflicting feelings? Besides, few of us can wipe out a nation as punishment for betrayal. Few of us can threaten that level of violence… and yet. There is something about the pain of great betrayal that can cry out for destruction of some sort. Of course our motivations are inevitably marred and mixed, but perhaps, while there are no easy answers to the thought of God bringing destruction to people he has made, we must remember that we are made in his image. We are made for relationship. We have to acknowledge the reality, as expressed by Jeremiah, of God's absolute agony in the face of his people's desertion. God's love is real.

....

Enjoy being loved by   Read John 3:16–17. Why did
God today.   God give his Son?

DA

The deal

'Reform your ways and your actions, and I will let you live in this place… If you really change your ways and your actions and deal with each other justly, if you do not oppress the alien, the fatherless or the widow and do not shed innocent blood in this place, and if you do not follow other gods to your own harm, then I will let you live… in the land I gave to your ancestors for ever and ever.'

Here it is again: Jeremiah is insisting, on the Lord's behalf, that change has to come. Some of the consequences of turning away from God are listed here: it had a knock-on effect on the way the people treated each other, too. They were not only treating God badly but abusing their neighbours as well. One sin was leading to another, and it had to stop. If it did—and here was the great thing—God promised that the future could be different. Punishment would not then be necessary. They could be kept safe and God would not need to use Babylon as a weapon of justice.

This was a wonderful offer of reprieve but it seems that it was never heeded enough. Jeremiah continued bringing the same message, even comparing the people's continued rebellion to adultery, but nothing was enough to cause nationwide repentance. No one wanted to know. It was all tied up with wanting to do their own thing, their own way, and not to acknowledge God any more.

In retrospect, it is very easy for us to condemn the Judeans for being so obtuse. How could they not respond when they had the amazing prophet right there with them? But if the choice that God puts before us is one between life and death, we would do better to examine our own lives and see where we are making the wrong choice ourselves. We have to take on board the truth that every choice we make will affect others as well as ourselves.

Dear Father, help me to choose you today in every area of my life.

Read Romans 6:15–23 to see some implications of your choice.

DA

The leaders

'A horrible and shocking thing has happened in the land: the prophets prophesy lies, the priests rule by their own authority, and my people love it this way. But what will you do in the end?'

Jeremiah certainly does not pull any punches. He says it like it is, and the passion God feels for his people pours through his words. A dominant theme throughout Jeremiah's writings is his condemnation of the leaders of Judah. The Lord is scathing about the leadership of the prophets, priests and scribes—for example, saying, 'I am against the prophets who steal from one another words supposedly from me' (23:30), and accusing them of lying for their own ends. He held them accountable for leading the people into flagrant sin. Moreover, the general populace colluded with this mismanagement, not wanting to hear anything uncomfortable or challenging. So poor Jeremiah was left with the task of trying to persuade kings to accept the inevitability of Babylonian attack while other so-called prophets attempted to shout him down. Hananiah was one false prophet who had a public run-in with Jeremiah, which resulted in Jeremiah prophesying—accurately—that Hananiah would soon die for attempting to lead people astray (ch. 28).

How do we know if a prophetic message is 'the word of the Lord' or not? It is a salutary lesson that the majority of a nation chose to believe what they wanted to, rather than face the consequences of the truth. It proved disastrous. What pain might they have avoided, had they been prepared to listen properly? The same challenging principles apply to us. According to Jeremiah, it is vital that we learn how to recognise God when he speaks and not block our ears with prejudice or reluctance, even—and especially—when we suspect that God might not be saying exactly what we want him to.

....

Be brave enough to pray that God will deal with anything in your life that would deafen you to hearing his word to you.

Read John 10:1–5 to discover an encouraging promise from Jesus.

DA

The lies

'Am I only a God nearby,' declares the Lord, 'and not a God far away? Who can hide in secret places so that I cannot see them?' declares the Lord. 'Do not I fill heaven and earth? … Let the prophets who have dreams tell their dreams, but let the one who has my word speak it faithfully.'

The trouble was that the leaders and people of Judah were so far into self-deception that they had lost any kind of decent theology. Not only were they determined to listen to false prophets, but they were also losing sight of what kind of God their Yahweh was. Judah was behaving like a child who puts her hands over her ears and sings when she does not want to listen. They were convincing themselves that God neither saw what happened nor particularly cared: 'The people are saying, "He will not see what happens to us"' (12:4). They allowed themselves to believe that everything was OK: 'The prophets keep telling them, "You will not see the sword or suffer famine. Indeed, I will give you lasting peace in this place"' (14:13). They preferred to believe these lies and refused to consider anything else. Through Jeremiah, the Lord attempted to remind them that he sees everything and is everywhere. He challenged their inadequate theology.

Of course, we as Christians have the immeasurable benefit of knowing that the Holy Spirit lives in us and will guide us into all truth, so our theology—our understanding of who God is—must be fine. Or is it? Like the issue of hearing and recognising the word of the Lord, learning about who God really is seems to be a lifelong process, with unexpected turns along the way. The more we try to pin God down to a neat formula, the more he seems to delight in jumping out of the box and calling to us from the other side of the room. As Jeremiah asserts, there is nowhere where God is not.

Dear Father, help me to get to know you as you really are, day by day. Amen

Read Acts 10 for an example of God refusing to be limited by our understanding.

DA

The hope

'Like clay in the hand of the potter, so are you in my hand, O house of Israel. If at any time I announce that a nation or kingdom is to be uprooted, torn down and destroyed, and if that nation I warned repents of its evil, then I will relent and not inflict on it the disaster I had planned.'

Jeremiah did make it clear that disaster was not a foregone conclusion. If only the people repented, then they would be protected. But the prophet was realistic enough to see that this just was not going to happen. The nation was too far gone in its idolatry. His advice to the kings was to submit to the Babylonians when they raged through the region, in order to limit the damage. The first of these kings was Josiah, usually credited with bringing in some reform to the land (2 Chronicles 34:33). Workmen in the temple had found a portion of the 'Book of the Law', which prompted Josiah to sweep out idolatrous objects from the temple and renew the covenant of Israel with Yahweh. However, this was clearly not enough. Perhaps the clue lies in Jeremiah 4:4: 'Circumcise yourselves to the Lord, circumcise your hearts, you people of Judah and inhabitants of Jerusalem.' Josiah may have changed the landscape, but it was a heart change that was really needed.

It's just the same for us. A smiling face on a Sunday is not what it takes to follow Jesus. It is easy, even in Christian circles, to pick up the language and the behaviour but not the love-relationship with Jesus. But God is not fooled by how we look on the outside. He knows whether we love him or not. He knows whether we have hearts that love him back and therefore try to obey him every day during the week. The Christian life is not a case of coercion or occasion for guilt. It is a relationship.

....

How do you know how much you love Jesus? How does it show in your life? How will your love for him grow?

Read 1 Corinthians 13 for a reminder of what love is.

DA

The scroll

Whenever Jehudi had read three or four columns of the scroll, the king cut them off with a scribe's knife and threw them into the brazier, until the entire scroll was burned in the fire. The king and all his attendants who heard all these words showed no fear... So Jeremiah took another scroll and gave it to the scribe Baruch son of Neriah, and as Jeremiah dictated, Baruch wrote.

Two kings later on, and Jeremiah was having trouble getting Jehoiakim to listen to him. Jeremiah was not allowed to go to the temple, so he sent his secretary friend, Baruch, instead. This time he wrote his message down for Jehoiakim. It was the same message as ever—a desperate plea for the king and his people to turn back wholeheartedly to God and so avoid punishment, along with prophecies about the coming catastrophe. It is interesting that Jehoiakim bothered to listen to the reading of the scroll: perhaps he did not dare treat it with complete contempt. When Jeremiah heard that Jehoiakim had burnt the whole thing, he dictated it all again, only this time a bit longer. Persistence was one of his key characteristics.

This was one of many interactions that Jeremiah had with the royal rulers. Others included being arrested, thrown into prison, thrown into a well and invited to secret meetings. God had called Jeremiah to a life not only of speech and potential political influence but also of prophetic actions—the visual aids of the day. For example, Jeremiah was asked by God to hide a linen belt in a crack in the rocks until it went rotten (13:1–7). Then he was asked to dig it out again, for 'as a belt is bound round someone's waist, so I bound... the whole house of Judah to me... But they have not listened' (v. 11). Thus God's heartbroken plea to his people was brought to life. Surely some people in the crowd that watched Jeremiah retrieve his ruined belt got the message?

....

What feeds your spiritual life?   Read John 15:1–17 to find
How can you get more of it?   Jesus' prescription for spiritual
                                           growth.

                                                                        DA

The survivors

'I have loved you with an everlasting love; I have drawn you with loving-kindness. I will build you up again and you will be rebuilt, O Virgin Israel. Again you will take up your tambourines and go out to dance with the joyful... Make your praises heard, and say, "O Lord, save your people, the remnant of Israel."'

As the story of Jeremiah progressed, the tone of his prophetic sayings began to change. There were still plenty of pronouncements of agonised, angry retribution for Judah's desertion, but they started to be balanced with passages of hope for restoration in the future. Some of the poetry of these promises is deeply moving as God's passion for his people shines through. Jeremiah anticipated a future beyond punishment and disaster and exile, and this future is full of hope and prosperity. Having labelled Judah's idolatry as adultery with other gods, now the survivors of the catastrophe are referred to as 'virgin'. It's as if the anger is spent and God's overwhelming longing for a restored people and a restored relationship is all that matters. He longs to forgive and 'remember their sins no more' (31:34). He will look after the remnant of his people like a caring shepherd (v. 10). God was never after annihilation. He always wanted resurrection.

There are obvious parallels here with the Gospel story, which I am sure I do not have to spell out. The only difference is that Jesus has now taken the punishment on himself so that we do not have to suffer it. It is worth digging into the whole of Jeremiah 31 for its powerful images of a loving, caring but still absolutely just God. If, by any chance, you are struggling with guilt over sin or stuck in a cycle of wrongdoing that seems stronger than you, allow God to speak to you through Jeremiah. Of course sin is desperately serious, but concentrate on how God wants things to be for his people, including you.

....

Give some time to chapter 31   Read Isaiah 49:13–16 to see
today. Don't hesitate to ask for   how much God loves you.
help if you need it. You matter.   DA

The new covenant

'This is the covenant I will make with the house of Israel after that time… I will put my law in their minds and write it on their hearts. I will be their God, and they will be my people. No longer will they teach their neighbours… "Know the Lord," because they will all know me.'

Like the rainbow and sunshine after the storm, the way that Jeremiah expressed what God has in store for his people brings a glorious relief. The darkness is over; the light has come. Sin is to be forgotten. Punishment and pain are done with. This is a new day. The covenant will be renewed, but it is not a revamped contract. It is an entirely new deal. This time God and his people will belong to each other completely. They will be so close that his law will be part of their DNA; it will not even need to be taught. Best of all, everyone will know God for themselves. After the challenge of prophesying judgment and destruction, it must have been a wonderful revelation for Jeremiah as he began to catch more of God's heart for a positive, blessed future.

This picture of God and humanity wrapped up in relationship together is what God was longing for all along. This was what he desired when he chose Israel in the first place. It was not the broken rules that called down judgment; it was God's broken heart.

As Christians, we should recognise from experience what Jeremiah was talking about here. We are the ones who have the extraordinary gift of the Holy Spirit, bringing to us exactly what Jeremiah foresaw. The Spirit is the one who changes us from the inside and reassures us of God's intimate presence with us. We can know total forgiveness. We can know God himself. We get to live the dream.

....

If there is anything that prevents you from enjoying the kind of relationship with God that Jeremiah described, just deal with it. Don't miss out. As encouragement, copy out Romans 15:13 and stick it where you can see it frequently.

DA

The purpose

'Take these documents, both the sealed and unsealed copies of the deed of purchase, and put them in a clay jar so they will last a long time. For this is what the Lord Almighty, the God of Israel, says: Houses, fields and vineyards will again be bought in this land… As I have brought all this great calamity on this people, so I will give them all the prosperity I have promised them.'

Yet again Jeremiah was asked by God to put his money where his mouth was. This time he was told to buy a field in Anathoth from his cousin Hanamel. Jeremiah obediently spent his 17 shekels of silver as a sign that the fall of Judah to Babylon would not be the end of the story. He gave the deeds in their clay jar to his friend Baruch, and made sure that his fellow Jews knew what he was doing. Thus he created a visual memory for them that he, at least, believed they would be back, despite the Babylonian siege ramps leaning against the city walls.

Jeremiah's faithfulness to God was rewarded by more promises of glorious restoration in the future, spurred on by God's passion (v. 41). For those who paid attention, these prophetic words and actions must have been extremely important to hang on to as they watched their city fall to the Babylonians. While later prophecies insisted that Babylon too would come under God's wrath for the pain it had inflicted, nevertheless it must have been traumatising to watch as the Babylonians stripped the land of people and the temple of treasures. I hope that some of the Jews remembered Jeremiah's clay jar…

We all have times when it is hard to believe that God purposes good in our lives. We too face loss, disruption and even despair. We need then to hang on to the promises of God that he knows what he is doing, yet feels the pain along with us. What is the equivalent for you of Jeremiah's clay jar?

....

Dear Father, please give me all I need to face the hard times. Thank you that you are my provider. Amen

Read Romans 8:28–39 to encourage your faith.

DA

The exile

'If you stay in this land, I will build you up and not tear you down; I will plant you and not uproot you, for I am grieved over the disaster I have inflicted on you. Do not be afraid of the king of Babylon, whom you now fear.'

Jerusalem had fallen by now, and King Nebuchadnezzar had appointed a governor of Judah, Gedaliah, to rule under his authority. Much of the population had been carried off to exile in Babylon, but a few remained. Some rebels assassinated Gedaliah, and the surviving Jews began a flight to Egypt, fearful of reprisals. Unsure of their choice, the fleeing group came to Jeremiah and asked him for God's word. Perhaps now that his message had been vindicated, Jeremiah was suddenly popular. Jeremiah was convinced that God was telling them to settle down in Babylon and trust that God would bring blessing to them even there. But the commanders of the party accused Jeremiah of lying, and dragged him and Baruch off to Egypt with them, where Jeremiah promised that eventual destruction awaited.

It is scary how consistent Jeremiah's contemporaries were in rejecting his prophecy, even after the Babylonian triumph. Jeremiah's words held solid advice for surviving in an alien land and reassured the people that God could bless them just as well there as anywhere else. Perhaps the Judeans already in Babylon heard of Jeremiah's encouraging promises from God.

God is not limited by our geographical situation or by our life situation. Sometimes life just does not turn out how we planned it to, or even how we thought God had planned it to. But his grace and good purposes can reach us wherever we are, whether we wanted to be there or not. He is a God of compassion and restoration for us, too. So be open to the word of the Lord, no matter how life is or where you are.

....

Come to us, Lord, and bless us.   Read Acts 8:1–8 for a picture of God working things together for good.

DA

The cost

The word of the Lord has brought me insult and reproach all day long. But if I say, 'I will not mention him or speak any more in his name,' his word is in my heart like a fire, a fire shut up in my bones. I am weary of holding it in; indeed, I cannot. I hear many whispering, 'Terror on every side! Report him! Let's report him!' … But the Lord is with me like a mighty warrior.

It is impossible to blame Jeremiah for his outburst in these verses. The poor man had just been beaten and put in stocks for a day for prophesying disaster—in the temple, no less. For a priest, it must have been especially hard to know that the person punishing him was a senior leader at the temple. So Jeremiah had a good moan to God about the rotten way he was always treated when he spoke the word of the Lord. As we come to the end of our time with Jeremiah, we cannot ignore the cost to the man of the words he has given to us.

For a start, he had no family, for God had told him not to marry, as a sign of the pointlessness of normal life when destruction was on the way (16:1–4). He did have some good friends—Baruch, for one—and those who supported him when he was threatened by the establishment, such as Ahikam (26:24). But he also had many enemies, especially among the false prophets and the later kings. This meant that his life was often threatened and he endured imprisonments, restrictions and ridicule. He cannot have been very popular, considering his persistent and challenging call to repentance.

Perhaps the hardest thing for him, however, was that he felt what God felt. He felt the pain, the longing, the despair, the vacillating anger and love—and once he had signed up for the job, there was no escaping the fire of God's word in his bones. His was a difficult calling. If only he could have known that we would find God in his words, many hundreds of years later.

....

Do you speak up for God, even when you might suffer for it? Pray for opportunities to make a difference in Jesus' name.

Read Acts 4:23–31 to see how Peter and John reacted to imprisonment.

DA

Fiona Barnard works with students from around the world. Her experiences have given her insights that will help us over the next two weeks as she helps us to appreciate the Bible as literature.

Jie from China was a student in the UK. She wanted to learn about British culture and believed Christianity to be a huge part of it, but she knew nothing about the Bible. She started at Genesis but, by mid-Exodus, when faced with rules for wilderness wandering, she gave up. Did Christians really believe in burnt offerings and stone tablets?

Jenny from Canterbury was a new Christian. At first she was enthusiastic about daily Bible reading but then she got bogged down in Corinthians. There were references to tongues and prophecies, women covering their heads in worship and people eating food sacrificed to idols. Jenny has concluded that it is totally irrelevant to her.

Jan from California has been a Christian for years. She knows the story of the Bible; however, there are vast parts into which she never ventures. She avoids the 'ranting' prophecies in the Old Testament. She is suspicious of 'fantastic' books like Daniel and Revelation. She jumps over lists of names and numbers. Although she would never admit it, the Bible she actually reads is a whole lot shorter than the 66-book version.

The timeless truths of God and his salvation are rooted in historical particularity. Written over 1500 years in cultures, places and times vastly different from our own, the Bible is a library. It contains history and story, biography and testimony, poetry and proverbs, lists and letters, law and lament. If we want to dig deep and discover the wonders of scripture, we have to consider the original context of the writing, including the type of literature it is and how the words would have been understood by the original hearers or readers. Then we need to ponder how they might apply to us. In these next two weeks, we will be exploring the different types of literature in this amazing, life-transforming word of God. May we recognise afresh that 'every part of Scripture is God-breathed and useful… Through the Word we are put together and shaped up for the tasks God has for us' (2 Timothy 3:16–17, THE MESSAGE).

Reading the start

First this: God created the Heavens and Earth—all you see, all you don't see. Earth was a soup of nothingness, a bottomless emptiness, an inky blackness. God's Spirit brooded like a bird above the watery abyss. God spoke: 'Light!' And light appeared. God saw that light was good and separated light from dark.

My mischievous friend spoiled the film *Billy Elliot* for me. At the very beginning, she whispered, 'He meets a sticky end.' As I hadn't read the publicity about this feel-good movie, I got myself ready to watch a tragedy. I experienced the whole story in the wrong frame of mind.

The beginning of any book sets the scene for us. It introduces the characters and themes. It provides the key to unravelling the plot. Genesis 1 opens in a blaze of poetry that starts with God: God initiates, creates, gives life and fills the world with goodness. The earth, along with the vegetables, animals, minerals and humans inhabiting it, are his wonderful idea, his amazing handiwork.

We're reminded at the start that humankind is not the centre of the universe: God is. Yet, in his overwhelming generosity, he shares creation with us, to enjoy and tend. He makes us like him in our ability to think and plan and be in relationship.

This book of beginnings also recounts our rebellion, our urge to be 'like God, knowing good and evil' (3:5, NIV). It shows the consequences of this terrible desire in broken relationships and violence, pride and self-seeking.

So the scene is set. Paradise is lost but the God who created order out of chaos makes and remakes. He calls imperfect individuals, and those who respond become part of his great rescue plan—that all the nations of the earth may be blessed. The plot of the Bible is inaugurated.

....

Forgive me, Lord, for considering how you can be part of my plans rather than how I am part of yours.

Read about Jesus' work in creation and recreation, in Colossians 1:15–23.

FVB

Reading the law

The Lord said to Moses, 'Speak to the entire assembly of Israel and say to them: "Be holy because I, the Lord your God, am holy… Do not seek revenge or bear a grudge against one of your people, but love your neighbour as yourself. I am the Lord."'

'Marriage is just about rules—putting the lid on the toothpaste and food on the table.' If that's your view, you may be a cynic or you may have overlooked the best that marriage can bring. Similarly, if you read the Old Testament laws (found mainly between Exodus and Deuteronomy) and conclude that what God required of his people was strict rule-keeping, you may have missed the heart of the matter.

Covenant lies at the centre of these laws. God rescued the people from slavery. He courted them and demonstrated his love by providing for them in the wilderness. When they agreed to be his people, they promised to honour him as their God. Then came the nitty-gritty. As we read through Leviticus 19, we find laws about parents, idols, sacrifice, harvesting crops, stealing, lying, care of people with disabilities, gossip, grudges, anger, revenge, foreigners and more. God was establishing a society to reflect his kindness, rather than one based on selfish ambition and greed.

'Will you love her, honour her, comfort and keep her as long as you both shall live?' When a dewy-eyed couple make their wedding vows, they don't resent the impossible demands made of them. They risk everything in a world of fickleness and selfishness because, in getting to know each other, loving trust has grown. The public promises provide a protective framework around frail human affection.

Washing up and keeping the household accounts are not everyone's delight but when we feel that by doing them we demonstrate our care and commitment to our spouse, the drudgery can be transformed. Then we understand God's plan for his covenant.

....

Remind me, Lord, when discipleship is hard, of all that you have done for me. Then help me to love you more.

Read John 14:23–27 to remind yourself of everything you have through the new covenant.

FVB

Reading wisdom

What is the best thing to do in the short life that God has given us? I think we should enjoy eating, drinking, and working hard… Life is short and meaningless, and it fades away like a shadow.

Chris couldn't believe in God or angels. He didn't cling to a wishful hope of an afterlife as he lay on his death bed. So his funeral in a crematorium and the champagne reception that followed celebrated his life—as a devoted husband, a successful academic, an enthusiastic sailor, a lover of good wine, a man of friendship with a discerning palate. By all accounts, he had lived well.

That 'goodbye' seemed very final and reflected something of the philosopher's outlook here in Ecclesiastes: enjoy life; get the most out of it, because death comes to good and bad alike and wipes it all away. This fatalism indicates a practical type of atheism, a life lived without any meaningful reference to God. It's the life choice of a huge number of people in the world: 'This is how I am going to live now, grabbing what happiness I can, because I can only be sure of today.'

Why is a book like this included in the Bible? It seems to go against so much of the rest of scripture's teaching. Well, that is precisely why it's there. It reminds us of the futility of chasing after material success and nothing else. It demonstrates the emptiness of living only for pleasure. It holds up a mirror to contemporary philosophy and asks, 'Is this it? Is this enough? Can this really satisfy?' Biblical wisdom reflects on daily realities for believers trying to make sense of it all.

The last words of the book come as a stark wake-up call: 'Respect and obey God! This is what life is all about. God will judge everything we do' (12:13–14).

....

Help me, Lord, to live by your values and priorities, so that what I do today will count for eternity.

Read Matthew 6:31–33 to see God's care and God's call on your life.

FVB

Reading proverbs

Train children in the way they should go, and when they are old they will not turn from it.

'Quick—I need help and I need it now!' In a world where we require wisdom but don't have time to acquire it, proverbs seem the perfect solution. They are short enough to fit on a cushion or calendar, funny enough to be enjoyable and memorable enough to be effective. No wonder the book of Proverbs has been popular with busy people.

The nuggets of advice are not always comfortable, though. I remember inward childhood groans when my mother mentioned ants and sluggards (6:6) in relation to an untidy bedroom or an incomplete task. As I grew older, dripping tap jokes (19:13) were no longer funny, and the good wife in Proverbs 31, who could do all things effortlessly, became someone I would never like to meet.

It is worth remembering that, although these biblical proverbs do contain truths, they don't enshrine the whole truth; nor are they theological statements. Showing how to behave well in the world, they give good advice, especially to young people. Exceedingly practical and pragmatic, their poetry and punch are often exaggerated and deliberately one-sided to make the point.

On the surface, today's verses might look like promises of reward for decency and punishment for foolishness. Yet we know that this is not always—not even often—the way things work in this life. Good parenting does not guarantee perfectly formed adult offspring. Respect for God does not automatically bring long life and wealth. This is why it is important that we balance proverbs with each other and read them in the light of the rest of scripture. Each is indeed a pearl, but a necklace needs many pearls. It must be held together by strong string and a firm clasp, encompassing the wider truth of the Bible and the lived-out experience of God's people.

Show me, Lord, how I might 'live well' today, not to gain celestial Brownie points but for your glory and honour.

FVB

Reading the parables

'One day someone came to visit the rich man, but the rich man didn't want to kill any of his own sheep or cattle and serve it to the visitor. So he stole the poor man's little lamb and served it instead.'

'Tell me a story!' Do we ever stop asking for stories? You don't have to be an avid reader or a soap devotee to be telling and listening to stories. If you share a home with others or rub shoulders with colleagues, if you keep in touch with friends or watch the news, if you write a diary or have dreams in your sleep, you know something about storytelling.

Stories get under your skin. You identify with particular people, feeling their happiness and pain, excitement and frustration. You enter another world. Your defences are down and you are free to see things differently. You are satisfied or outraged or surprised by the story's conclusion.

David had just taken another man's wife and had him killed. As far as he was concerned, he was king and could do what he wanted. He had covered his tracks and would have countered anyone who challenged him. It was the story of a pet lamb, adored by a poor man and his children, that shattered his defences. He was furious: how could the rich man, who had so many sheep, steal the one little lamb from that heartbroken family?

'You are that rich man!' replied the prophet Nathan, and immediately David recognised his wrongdoing: 'I have disobeyed the Lord' (v. 13). Suddenly, he felt the emotional impact of what he had done, and could grasp the huge injustice of his self-serving actions. The pet lamb had reached him in a way that sermons rarely can.

Parables, like advertisements, are meant to elicit a response in the hearer. Have you stolen someone's pet lamb recently? Have you mistreated something or someone precious in pursuit of your own ends?

....

Lord Jesus, thank you that you love me enough to show me where I have hurt you. Please open my eyes, and forgive me!

Read Luke 15:1–7 for another sheepy tale.

FVB

Reading poetry

Listen, God! Please, pay attention! Can you make sense of these ramblings, my groans and cries? King-God, I need your help… Every morning I lay out the pieces of my life on your altar and watch for fire to descend.

What do I do with the pain when my friend lets me down or an illness rages through my body? Where can I put the anguish and anger when colleagues whisper against me or when a project that gave me great satisfaction is snatched away? Where do I go when someone who promised to love me betrays me and it seems as though God himself has disappeared?

Poetry has been a medium, over the centuries, through which people have poured out their hearts on paper, in song and in prayer. It allows us to express something of our crushing, larger-than-life emotions—and in 'getting it out' we find a measure of relief.

By including laments and songs of thanksgiving, hymns of praise and songs of trust, salvation-history psalms, wisdom psalms and songs of celebration, the Bible expresses the whole rainbow of human emotion and experience. Individuals and whole communities respond to the unfolding of life. God is part of it all and dignifies our cries of agony and ecstasy by including them in his word.

Sometimes we can feel guilty about the strength of our feelings, especially if they are negative ones towards other people. Yet those who wrote and then prayed the psalms, including Psalm 5, incorporated their fury in their prayers. Perhaps they were saved from sin by handing the need for revenge over to God.

I may feel as though my life is in bits, shattered by circumstances or cruelty. There is something very beautiful in the picture of coming to God with the broken pieces of my life, laying them out before him and waiting for him to transform them, somehow, into a sacrifice.

Write your own psalm to God today.

If you are finding it hard to praise God, use the words of Psalm 146.

FVB

Reading the prophets

'I will write my laws on their hearts and minds. I will be their God, and they will be my people. No longer will they have to teach one another to obey me… I will forgive their sins and forget the evil things they have done.'

Toothache, hunger pangs, bathroom scales and mock exams all jog me to take action. They remind me of dental check-ups or lunch; they warn about too much chocolate and not enough study. Important matters can slip away in the busyness of life: the things that shout most loudly for attention are not always true priorities. I need prompts to remind me to care for vital issues of well-being.

The biblical prophets were like that. Mostly active between 760 and 460BC, their role was to remind God's people of their promises to him, and his promises to them, as they built homes and families, traded in the marketplaces and faced threats from foreign powers. Out of gratitude, they had agreed to follow his ways. They were to embody his goodness and care.

They had short memories, though. They were preoccupied and anxious. They were attracted to more exciting religions. God's way was too hard and they were unfaithful—so God sent prophets. We have 16 collections of their words as Old Testament books, expressing sorrow and love, anger and pleading.

Everything we read in the prophets is tied to specific historical situations, which can make it hard to interpret for ourselves. Nevertheless, here in Jeremiah, we can rejoice with the Israelites not only that our sins can be forgiven but also that, by God's Spirit, we know how to please the Lord. His laws are not 'out there' but in our hearts. By his grace, we want to please him, and when we don't, forgiveness is available through Christ.

....

What reminders do you need today about God's priorities for your life?

For one of God's priorities, read Micah 6:8.

FVB

Reading narrative

'Do not think that because you are in the king's house you alone of all the Jews will escape… And who knows but that you have come to royal position for such a time as this.'

Mid-life crisis, for me, meant blowing out 40 candles and wondering what on earth I had done with my life. Weighing all my idealistic longings and determination to change the world for Jesus against the reality of a very unspectacular life left me gloomy, to say the least. How did my boring story fit in with God's magnificent story?

Interestingly, the Bible spends a lot of time dealing with just such a question. Over 40 per cent of the Old Testament is story—told on three levels. It describes the unfolding of God's universal plan, the account of Israel's history, and the telling of many individual narratives. Take, for example, the beautifully crafted story of Esther. This young, submissive Jewish girl is chosen to be queen, wife of a foreign despot. We hold our breath as she is burdened with the responsibility of pleading for the lives of her ethnic-minority people, who are to be exterminated by the egocentric Haman. We marvel as she blossoms into a woman of authority and nerve.

The beauty treatment, the whispered messages between her cousin and servants, and the banquets prepared for her husband and Haman are the details of Esther's life, which have huge consequences for the Jews—indeed, for their very survival. These incidents are also part of God's sovereign plan as he preserves a people from whom Jesus, the Saviour of the world, will be descended.

Poignantly, the name of God never appears in the book, and yet his presence is everywhere. We may feel very insignificant and unaware of God's activity but we can be encouraged that, as God's children, we are part of his story, which one day we will be told in full.

···

Lord, help me not to be so caught up in my own story that I forget the greater narrative you are weaving in the world.

Read Luke 1:26–38 for another story of a woman whose costly 'yes' changed history.

FVB

Reading genealogies

Jesus Christ came from the family of King David and also from the family of Abraham. And this is a list of his ancestors… Judah and his brothers (Judah's sons were Perez and Zerah, and their mother was Tamar)… Boaz (his mother was Rahab), Obed (his mother was Ruth)… Solomon (his mother had been Uriah's wife)… Joseph, the husband of Mary, the mother of Jesus, who is called the Messiah.

Lists can be very boring, unless you spot a familiar name—a prize winner in a competition, an actor in a play or a guest at a meal. Most people are glad that film credits roll quickly, but the doting mothers of the sound recordist or the stunt driver read every word to glimpse their loved one's name. It all depends on perspective.

Our society is becoming fascinated with genealogies as research becomes easier. We are beginning to realise what many cultures throughout the world have understood for millennia—that our identity is caught up in our history. Somehow we know who we are better when we know where we have come from.

The genealogies in the Bible carry treasures that impatience can cause us to miss. Matthew 1 is not just an assortment of names. It grounds Jesus in history. It places him as a true Jew—a descendant of Abraham, the hero and father of the Jewish faith. Jesus is also the true Messiah, the promised one in the line of King David. His coming is the climax of Jewish longing.

Shockingly, there is no attempt to hide skeletons in cupboards. David's adultery, the murder of Uriah, the deceit of Judah and Tamar and the wickedness of Manasseh are almost underlined. Jesus identifies with sinful humanity. Unusually for a patriarchal society, four women are included, all probably non-Jews. Faithful Ruth from Moab and pragmatic Rahab from Jericho are no longer outsiders. They are integral to the family. In Christ, there is a place for all.

....

Thank you, Lord, that I'm not just an insignificant name on a list. I'm part of your family of sinners and saints. Hallelujah!

FVB

Reading the Gospels

Mary was engaged to Joseph from King David's family... When Jesus was born... Herod was king. During this time some wise men from the east came to Jerusalem and said, 'Where is the child born to be king of the Jews? We saw his star in the east and have come to worship him.'

'Why have you come from Japan to do a PhD in the UK?' I asked Poro. We were enjoying soup and sushi soon after he'd arrived. 'During the Second World War,' he replied, 'the Japanese were required to show their allegiance by worshipping the emperor. Some Christians wavered and complied; others resisted and died. I have come to study what Matthew says about Jesus as king, so that when we are in that situation again, I will have prepared my congregation.'

Poro referred to this passage, where God inaugurates his kingdom on earth. Jesus, descended from King David, is king of the Jews. He is also worshipped by wise foreign 'pagans'. Fearing political threat, King Herod tries to destroy Jesus but God saves the Saviour through Joseph.

Why do four Gospels tell more or less the same story of Jesus' life? These 'memoirs of the apostles' recall what Jesus said and did—but the accounts were selected and shaped with particular communities in mind. 'Remember that God is sovereign and only Jesus is Lord—even when it doesn't feel like it!' That's Matthew's message to persecuted believers, so he includes Jesus' promise: 'When someone arrests you, don't worry... you will be given the words to say... They can kill you, but they cannot harm your soul' (10:19, 28).

Many early Christians faced martyrdom for denying that Caesar was Lord. How comforting for the original readers to know that Jesus understood! What a challenge for persecuted Christians today to confess that only Jesus is Lord!

....

I may not face severe persecution, but how do I acknowledge Jesus as king in my daily life?

You could use 2 Corinthians 1:2–11 to pray for Christians facing persecution.

FVB

Reading history

Jesus… said, 'Everything is done!' He bowed his head and died… We know this is true, because it was told by someone who saw it happen… Mary Magdalene then went and told the disciples that she had seen the Lord.

This Good Friday, Jing from China came to an all-age service. She had never been to church before and was trying to make sense of what she was hearing. Over coffee and hot cross buns, I struggled to explain what seems like the 'unfairness' of Jesus dying in our place, taking the punishment for our sins. After I'd spoken as clearly as I could for a few minutes, she asked, 'But did Jesus exist in history?'

Our Christian faith stands or falls on certain historical facts. If the Gospel accounts in the Bible are just good stories, we are complete fools for living our lives for Jesus. If it is all a figment of someone's imagination, we are wasting our time.

Non-biblical historians confirm that Jesus lived and died. The Gospel writers describe what happened based on the testimony of eyewitnesses, and those who wrote the epistles explain, on reflection, the meaning of the events: 'Christ died once for our sins. An innocent person died for those who are guilty. Christ did this to bring you to God' (1 Peter 3:18).

What about the resurrection? Isn't that incredible? The early disciples certainly thought so. The Gospel accounts acknowledge their bewilderment and fear: this was not what they were expecting. Yet the empty tomb, the absence of a body, the encounters of the risen Jesus with different people and their transformed lives, all point to something astonishing: Jesus really did rise from the dead. His bodily resurrection not only confirms that God has accepted his sacrifice but also points to our future hope. Death is not the end of life.

....

Lord, I am staking my life on you. You died to forgive my sin. You rose from death because you are the Lord of life.

FVB

Reading testimony

'As I came near Damascus, suddenly a bright light from heaven flashed around me. I fell to the ground and heard a voice say to me, "Saul! Saul! Why do you persecute me?" "Who are you, Lord?" I asked. "I am Jesus of Nazareth, whom you are persecuting", he replied.'

'I was there. I saw it. I heard it. It was like this…' There is something utterly compelling about personal testimony, whether from a witness to an accident, a journalist in a distant land or a Christian speaking of God's intervention in her life. We sit up. We take note. This is real.

When Luke wrote the history of the early Church in Acts, he did not produce a dry, dusty account of statistics, dates and principles of ecclesiastical governance. He gave an account of how God the Holy Spirit revolutionised the lives of native and Greek-speaking Jews in Jerusalem, as well as Samaritans, Gentiles and people at 'the ends of the earth'.

Fascinatingly, the passages beginning 'we' underline the fact that Luke is not relying on hearsay, years after the events. He travelled with Paul and saw what happened. If he wasn't present, he knew those who were and made sure he took note of the details.

So we read how Luke was there to hear Paul narrate his conversion as the crowds bayed for his blood. Paul recalls his persecution of Christians, and then the moment when God intervened, not only to change the course of his life but also to give him the special task of telling the nations about Jesus.

Each of us has our own unique story. We can't conclude, just because we didn't experience lights and voices, that our encounter with Jesus was deficient. God deals with us in different ways. The important thing is that our sins have been washed away as we called on his name (v. 16) and that our lives are facing Godward.

....

'Always be prepared to… give the reason for the hope that you have' (1 Peter 3:15, NIV). Practise so that you're ready!

Read 2 Corinthians 12:7–9 for another testimony of God's power in the face of weakness.

FVB

Reading letters

I beg you to help Onesimus! He is like a son to me because I led him to Christ here in jail. Before this, he was useless to you, but now he is useful both to you and to me… To me he is a dear friend, but to you he is even more, both as a person and as a follower of the Lord.

I remember trying to decipher my father's handwriting. Did it really say 'Keep the mince to yourself'? And if so, what did it mean? Correspondence between the UK and Brazil in the early 1980s could take up to ten days each way, so sometimes I received comments on remarks I'd forgotten I'd made. It was only some time later that I remembered spilling some dinner on the envelope and writing 'Here is some mince' next to the smudge.

It's worth noting that the 21 letters in the New Testament are each only one half of a conversation, separated from us by time and geography. Written to individuals and churches, they emerged from very particular situations, relationships and challenges. It is dangerous to draw timeless principles for church practice from the text when we don't know the whole historical context. Yet we can't dismiss them as historical curiosities because they are still God's word.

On the face of it, what is the relevance to us of a very personal letter between friends, asking a slave owner to welcome back an escapee rather than have him killed as an example to others? We don't have slaves: we believe slavery is wrong.

Our society still values hierarchy and status and power. It's easy to fall into the trap of comparing ourselves with others and considering some people more worthy of our notice. The church is no place for titles and name-dropping. Paul's letter emphasises equality: each Christian is 'a person and a follower'. While Paul did not campaign against slavery, this revolutionary belief in a common humanity in Christ undermined the practice.

....

Paul's letter demonstrates God's particular care for individuals and relationships. Is there a letter, email or call you can send today to demonstrate his love?

FVB

Reading apocalyse

I am John, a follower together with all of you. We suffer because Jesus is our king, but he gives us the strength to endure. I was sent to Patmos island, because I had preached God's message... The Spirit took control of me... I heard a loud voice... 'Write in a book what you see. Then send it to the seven churches.'

Every week, I walk along hotel corridors cluttered with broken furniture, coffee urns and busy noticeboards. I spend two hours in a stuffy, windowless room teaching English to exhausted, low-paid overseas staff. They have worked at boring jobs since early morning and they live in a world where they don't really belong, not least because of the language barriers. I can almost feel the sense of hopelessness. Sometimes we have to use another room in the hotel, and en route we meet another world: the one the guests inhabit. Opulence and grandeur and comfort hit me. It is like a parallel universe, where, for a second, an open door gives me a glimpse into other possibilities.

Revelation is an open door into a realm we don't see. Its apocalyptic visions, its symbolism and cryptic language, familiar in the first century, can bemuse us today. Many unhelpful interpretations and preoccupation with detail have distracted Christians from the letter's intent: to encourage downhearted, weary, persecuted believers to persevere. How? By feeding their imagination. John, himself imprisoned for his faith, sees visions of the crucified, conquering Jesus; he witnesses heaven open, brimming with multicultural worship; he observes the judgment and defeat of God's enemies; he admires the new heaven and earth where there is no pain and God is present.

'Look at this! Have a peep!' John writes. 'Let these fantastic images help renew your commitment to Christ. He has suffered like you but is now triumphant. There is so much more behind the scenes. God is in control.'

Lord, when the discouragements of my life make me want to give up, remind me of your eternal certainties and keep me faithful.

Let the broad brushstrokes of your future destination encourage you: read Revelation 21:1–7.

FVB

Sandra Wheatley introduces the theme of the last set of notes in this series.

Our lives begin with the most hazardous journey, from the womb to the world. From there on we never really stop journeying and, as Christians, it is in the 'journey' that our lives in Christ are formed—even if we don't venture beyond our own street. Each day we embark on a journey that has little to do with physical distance and everything to do with our relationship with God.

Yet, at this time of year, we so often need a break from the busyness and stress of life. It may be a holiday, a trip of a lifetime or simply a break at home, away from those everyday pressures that can grind us down. We may need just a change of routine and some time to 'be'.

The Bible tells many stories of many journeying peoples. They had reasons similar to ours today for travelling and relocating. Not many would have seen their trips as 'holidays' (despite the word's original meaning as a time set apart to recognise or celebrate a festival), but we can still learn much from their experiences of finding God wherever they travelled, under whatever circumstances.

My travelling days are hampered now. To embark on any trip requires planning of almost military precision as wheelchairs, pressure-relieving mattresses and various other pieces of equipment accompany me. I may not travel often, but my 'journey' is far from over.

Physical restrictions don't dampen a spirit that still knows what it is to soar like an eagle and delight in knowing that, regardless of the harshness of the path, we are guaranteed a safe arrival. If you have time during this holiday period to rest a little longer and relax a little more, may the coming days bring the restoration and renewal you need as you meet with God through his word.

Leaving home

So the Lord God banished them from the Garden of Eden, and he sent Adam out to cultivate the ground from which he had been made. After sending them out, the Lord God stationed mighty cherubim to the east of the Garden of Eden.

Adam and Eve were settled and secure in the garden, with all that they needed, but they blew it. With everything that God had given and provided for them, it was their use of choice and free will that would be their downfall. Reading through this chapter shows us just how easy it is for any of us to be tempted and fall, and even to doubt what God has said.

They were to be banished and forcibly ejected from paradise, which was all they had known, with the way back barred by armed and very dangerous cherubim. This is the first recorded journey in the Bible. There was no packing or preparation, no planning of route or destination: they simply went 'east', into a harsh life of working the soil and providing for themselves.

It's hard to imagine their sense of loss. Their choice had set a seal on the gulf that opened up between God and humankind, and made necessary God's plan of redemption to draw each of us back to himself—although that would take thousands of years to come to fulfilment. Yet one final thing happened before Adam and Eve were banished that gives us a picture of God's eternal love and provision. God himself made garments of animal skins and clothed them (v. 21). A sacrifice was made to provide protection for them. Blood was shed for the first time in the Bible.

God clothed them and made sure they were ready—just as any parent would do in buttoning up the jacket of a child as they left for their first day at school. The saddest of journeys had begun but they were still clothed and protected by God. He wouldn't be far away.

....

Father God, the human story begins with such disaster and yet you still gave your all to win us back. Thank you!

SW

A journey by faith

It was by faith that Abraham obeyed when God called him to leave home and go to another land… He went without knowing where he was going.

Abram left his home and clan in a world where such actions were simply not done. Only the poverty-stricken or the defeated would wander; only the landless and the fugitives would move about and leave their ancestral homes. But God's words to Abram commanded him to leave everything and go to a place that God would not even describe until he got there.

We are told no details about the journey itself—but it must have been very difficult, as Abram didn't travel light (Genesis 12:5), and it was all 'by faith'. There were no National Express coaches, Virgin trains or easyJet planes, and no satellite navigation.

Exactly what was it that enticed Abram to embark on this journey? A promise—that's all. But what a promise (Genesis 12:2–3)! Just as Eve wasn't totally aware of the horrendous implications of her action in taking the forbidden fruit, maybe Abram wasn't aware of the glorious implications of his accepting God's promise. In responding as he did, by faith, Abram began the journey that would bring us all back to God, and set in motion the fulfilment of God's promise in Jesus and his death on the cross for us all.

Abram set off into the unseen, trusting his unknown future to a known God. His response is still an example to me, even now. It's a paradox, but it is better to walk with God in the dark than without him in the light, and better to walk by faith with him than to walk alone by sight.

You may be journeying with an unmet promise. Be encouraged as you read this story. Your time will come!

....

Dear Lord, please help us to live the little picture when we can't see the big picture, and to learn to trust you, no matter what you ask of us.

SW

A testing journey

'Take your son, your only son—yes, Isaac, whom you love so much—and go to the land of Moriah. Go and sacrifice him as a burnt offering on one of the mountains, which I will show you.' … On the third day of their journey, Abraham looked up and saw the place in the distance.

Abraham embarked on this journey without a question on his lips—but, I would imagine, with all sorts of emotions reeling around his head and heart. Everything God had promised Abraham was epitomised in Isaac. He was the fulfilment of the promise that had drawn Abraham from his ancestors and lands. Along the way there had been a 'detour' with Hagar and Ishmael (Genesis 16), but now the reality had arrived. Yet here they were, Abraham and the promised son, journeying together to Mount Moriah—once more in obedience to God, once more into the unknown.

Jerusalem would later be built upon this area—with Calvary just outside the city. That's a link worth remembering, but there are other comparisons for us to draw. I am reminded of some of the issues, people, hurts and disappointments that have needed to be taken to my own personal Moriah and laid on an altar of sacrifice. You may be facing such a journey at this time. I have done so recently.

To take something or someone that we hold very dear but has now become too much of a distraction from the things God would have us do and be, and give it up to God, seems almost impossible. It may be good—but is it the best for us? Whatever—or whomever—you are journeying with to your Moriah, may your grip on them lessen as you go, and may their grip upon you ease. These journeys of faith are our ultimate test, too, and none is taken lightly. Your obedience to God, your faith in him and your trust that he will provide for you will bear rich rewards. Trust him—it will be worth it.

....

Sometimes we need to lose what we cannot keep, to gain what we cannot lose.

SW

Companionship

But Ruth replied, 'Don't ask me to leave you and turn back. Wherever you go, I will go; wherever you live, I will live. Your people will be my people, and your God will be my God. Wherever you die, I will die, and there I will be buried. May the Lord punish me severely if I allow anything but death to separate us!'

If you can read the earlier verses in this chapter, they will give the background to why these two women, a mother- and daughter-in-law, are setting out on this grief-laden journey.

Naomi no longer had a reason to stay in Moab: everyone she loved had died. So she made the decision to return to her home in Bethlehem. Broken, lonely and fragmented in her spirit, she prepared to leave alone—but Ruth wouldn't let her. The words she spoke are among the most moving in scripture. They reveal a depth of care and companionship that bound these women together and set the seal on their journey and lives.

So many of us live 'alone'—even if we do share our homes with others. The pressures of life can force us into isolation, into a self-protective bubble where no one can touch us, let alone harm us; but we need companionship. We need to know that at least one other person on this planet is aware of our existence, and cares.

I have lived alone for almost 30 years—a 'spinster of the parish' who certainly knows how to spin! Perhaps that's why my appreciation of my friends is so deep and why, despite living alone, I never feel lonely. I simply cannot walk this path without their care and encouragement.

If you are at a stage or season in your life when the journey ahead seems stark and lonely, please look around for a friend, a companion who can join you in your travels.

....

A Swedish saying: 'Shared joy is a double joy. Shared sorrow is half a sorrow.' May you know the warmth of companionship, always.

SW

A return trip

But Samuel, though he was only a boy, served the Lord. He wore a linen garment like that of a priest. Each year his mother made a small coat for him and brought it to him when she came with her husband for the sacrifice… Meanwhile, Samuel grew up in the presence of the Lord.

This is a small and seemingly insignificant journey that a mother undertakes each year to see her son. My heart goes out to Hannah, whose story unfolds from chapter 1. The vow she makes to God (1:11) is so moving. The depth of her yearning for a son is immense, but so too is her devotion to God in being willing to give him back. That devotion and the sacrificial gift to God of her longed-for son continue to challenge me each time I read about her.

Samuel was only three years old when she left him. I'm not sure I could have done what Hannah did, but there is something precious in this story for us all—even today. Each year she made him a little coat and took it with her as she returned to the temple to make her sacrifice. When Hannah returned each year, the coat she made would have been that little bit bigger. Year upon year, her little boy would be growing into a young man. Hannah's journey each year wasn't to go back to see a little boy but to watch a growing man.

Many of us will remember a significant and memorable time when we dedicated our life to God. If we were to go back to that moment and see the life we dedicated as being still the same as it is now, then we'd have cause for concern.

Where I am now in my walk with God is, thankfully, very different from where I was last year or the year before. Progress may have been painfully slow, but there has been some growth.

Perhaps you might take an annual journey of the heart—to see what growth there has been and rejoice in what God has done and still is doing.

SW

A lonely road

[Elijah] went to Beersheba, a town in Judah, and he left his servant there. Then he went on alone into the desert, travelling all day. He sat down under a solitary broom tree and prayed that he might die, 'I have had enough, Lord,' he said. 'Take my life.'

Elijah was a mighty and powerful prophet: the previous chapters of 1 Kings show that his life had been lived at a breakneck speed. Yet the threats of a formidable woman drove him to the limits of depression and despair and sent him on this journey alone into a desert. Sometimes our journeys take us to very dark and lonely places.

'I've had enough, Lord' (v. 4). Have you ever said those words? I have—at times as a result of hurt and upset but, more recently, from the depths of despair and depression as intractable pain grows increasingly worse. One aspect of MS, and other neurological diseases, is chronic pain. The nervous system seems to go into overdrive and even the gentlest of touches can feel like a searing burn. I was prescribed opioids and anti-nausea drugs, which did nothing for the pain but sent me on a downward spiral, emotionally and psychologically. Added to that, I faced being evicted from my home by a ruthless and uncaring landlord.

Wave upon wave of depression and a sense of utter futility would hit me unexpectedly and I felt as if I couldn't go on. Like Elijah, I journeyed alone into a desert place and found myself asking God to take my life. But he didn't. Instead he sheltered me with friends and their prayers—just like Elijah's broom tree.

Paul's words, 'I have kept the faith' (2 Timothy 4:7, NIV), steadied me as I lived one hour at a time, saying, 'I have kept the faith for one more hour'—and then another, and another, until finally the depression and darkness passed. Once again I looked to God and said, 'Take my life', no longer out of desperation but from devotion.

....

Father God, when our paths become dark and foreboding, help us to feel your presence, somehow.

SW

The journey back

'I will go home to my father and say, "Father, I have sinned against both heaven and you, and I am no longer worthy of being called your son. Please take me on as a hired servant."' So he returned home to his father.

There are two journeys in this story. The first is the one *away* from home. The younger son had it all, but it wasn't enough. He demanded his inheritance and off he went to a 'distant land' (v. 13), to a new life, away from all constraints. The second journey is the return home. Starving and broken, destitute and shamed, the young man heads home and, with every step, rehearses his apology to his father—over and over again, uncertain what his reception will be. Many of us will have undertaken these two journeys. The first seems easy; the second is possibly one of the most difficult we'll ever make.

We have all seen someone else slip and stray and have tried to persuade them to stay where it is safe, in 'the Father's house'. Or perhaps you yourself have taken that journey to a distant land, where life seems more attractive than in the place where you were.

If you're on the journey homeward, guilt-ridden and broken by your experiences away from the Lord, needing his love and forgiveness as you struggle with the things you have done, not daring to hope that he will forgive you in an instant—then look again at the Father's reaction (vv. 20–22). The father runs to meet his wayward son. This is the only recorded kiss that God (as represented by the father) ever gives to anyone in the Bible. Here, our picture of God as cool, calm and collected is completely overturned. No heart beat hastier, no feet ran swifter, no embrace was stronger, no eyes were more watery and no kiss was firmer than this Father's. He had no face to save, no reputation to protect and no love to hide. His son was back.

....

This is the welcome you will receive—always.

SW

The journey to the tomb

Very early on Sunday morning, just at sunrise, [the women] went to the tomb. On the way they were asking each other, 'Who will roll away the stone for us from the entrance to the tomb?'

The women who had watched Jesus die now come to the tomb. They come in the dark, in the cold of early morning. They come to anoint Jesus' body and prepare it for its final rest. There will be no reward, no recognition. They can't bring him back to life, but they can still give him the gift they have bought and brought.

These women came. Peter wasn't there; Andrew hadn't jumped up and offered to help. The many people Jesus had healed were nowhere to be found; nor were the ones whose sins he had forgiven.

On the way to the tomb it seems as if they suddenly remembered about the huge stone that had been rolled across the entrance. In a moment they could have abandoned their journey and gone home. That would have been understandable—the stone was huge—but they carried on, undaunted and determined to perform this one last service to their Lord. So, on the morning of the resurrection, before they knew that the tomb was empty, these precious women came.

The story of this journey is for all of you who bring all that you have to God in service to him in out-of-the-way places, in the 'dark', where no one sees or knows. Your giving to the Lord in your service to his people is costly to you, but you don't ever let on. You stay when others leave; you clear up and make things comfortable for others.

You constantly 'anoint his body' as you serve the church and the people around you. All of this you do in the dark, out of sight of others and undaunted by any obstacles. You do what you do because you love him truly and deeply.

....

Women of God, I salute you! May you know the smile of his presence today as you journey on in service for him.

SW

The Emmaus journey

Now that same day two of them were going to a village called Emmaus, about seven miles from Jerusalem. They were talking with each other about everything that had happened... '... But we had hoped that he was the one who was going to redeem Israel.'

Same day, different journey. The women had earlier made their journey to the tomb; these two disciples were heading away from Jerusalem, downcast because of all they had seen. 'We had hoped...' they said. Now their hope was dead and buried, and, despite what the women had said about an empty tomb, they still left for Emmaus. The disappointment in these three words is tangible and recognisable to any who have been on the journey of faith for any length of time.

Recently I've undergone at least one operation a month for over seven months to implant a device in my abdomen with a catheter into my spinal cord, into which a local anaesthetic was injected to stop my pain. Sadly, it hasn't worked. I had hoped—hoped, after years of excruciating pain—that the answer had been found, but it wasn't to be.

I've had many a walk to 'Emmaus'. Our 'Emmaus' could be anywhere away from the place that has become unbearable. We try to get away from an experience that has left us wounded or left our longings unfulfilled, a potential not reached, dreams dashed. We can escape for a time from the hurt we felt or the hurt we caused, from the guilt that still nags at us and the disappointment that still rankles.

As we journey, though, Jesus comes to join us. We may not recognise him at once, but he stays with us, keeping step with us, listening to our heart's cry. Gently, hope is reignited by his presence. It is for me: the God of hope keeps pouring his oil on to the flame of my hope and keeps it alive in me. He hasn't failed me so far, and I know he never will.

....

Father God, ignite hope again in those whose lives are bruised or broken by disappointments.

SW

Coming home

Then Jesus said, 'Come to me, all of you who are weary and carry heavy burdens, and I will give you rest. Take my yoke upon you. Let me teach you, because I am humble and gentle at heart, and you will find rest for your souls.'

We started our journey through the scriptures by seeing Adam and Eve banished from the garden, and now we hear Jesus saying, 'Come to me.' Their journey has been matched step by step by God, drawing human beings back into relationship with himself. These words bring an invitation to each of us: 'Come to me.'

It is one more journey. It may be the first of many steps you'll take as you embark on your journey of faith. It may be a tentative step, but he'll take your hand and hold you steady. It may be a return journey to lay down your burdens, cares and worries. It may be a reluctant journey, because you want to keep going at the same pace, for fear that if you stop you may not get started again.

When I was newly diagnosed with MS and struggling to let go of the things I once did, I remembered the long summer days of my childhood and the battle my mum used to have with me, at the end of each day, to get me to come home. My brother and sister were very compliant, but I would run out of the back door again as quickly as I'd run through the front door. I just wanted to play outside a little longer. The nightly chase was on, and the neighbours would watch with glee as I so often outran my mum around the terrace of houses.

It seemed as if God was saying, 'It's time to come home. You've been playing out all day, but I want you to come home now, to be with me.' He didn't chase. There was no need: it was time to come home.

The greatest journey any of us will ever take isn't a geographical one; it is a spiritual one—the journey to him.

....

The invitation to come back to God is open to all. Jesus says, 'Come to me.'

SW

Other Christina Press titles

Women Celebrating Faith edited by Lucinda McDowell (£5.99)

A challenging collection of writings by women from all walks of life, taking time to look back on their lives at forty. No matter what age the reader is, they will be encouraged by the experiences of these women.

Dear God, It's Me and It's Urgent Marion Stroud (£6.99)

The beauty and depth of these prayers for women makes them unforgettable. The fact that they are rooted in everyday life gives them universal appeal.

In His Time Eileen Gordon-Smith (£5.99)

Five missionaries and seven children are killed in a bus crash. Where is God when it hurts? 'I am different now—I no longer fear death.'

Who'd Plant a Church? Diana Archer (£5.99)

Planting an Anglican church from scratch, with a team of four—two adults and two children—is an unusual adventure even in these days. Diana Archer gives a distinctive perspective on parish life.

Pathway Through Grief edited by Jean Watson (£6.99)

Ten Christians, each bereaved, share their experience of loss. Frank and sensitive accounts offering comfort and reassurance to those recently bereaved and new insights to those involved in counselling.

God's Catalyst Rosemary Green (£8.99)

Insight, inspiration and advice for both counsellors and concerned Christians who long to be channels of God's Spirit to help those in need. A unique tool for the non-specialist counsellor.

Angels Keep Watch Carol Hathorne (£5.99)

After 40 years, Carol Hathorne obeyed God's call to Kenya. She came face to face with dangers, hardships and poverty, but experienced the joy of learning that Christianity is still growing in God's world.

Not a Super-Saint Liz Hansford (£6.99)

Describes the outlandish situations that arise in the Manse, where life is both fraught and tremendous fun. A book for the ordinary Christian who feels they must be the only one who hasn't quite got it together.

Other BRF titles

Growing a Caring Church Wendy Billington (£6.99)

In every church, meeting people's pastoral needs is a core area of ministry. If leadership resources are already stretched, however, it is easy to fall short. Earthed in Jesus' command to love one another, this book shows how home groups can be places where people's difficulties are noticed, and first steps taken to help. Wendy Billington offers valuable insights and down-to-earth advice, drawing on her years of pastoral work and her own experiences of loss and cancer.

The Circle of Love Ann Persson (£5.99)

The painting of the Holy Trinity by Russian artist Andrei Rublev is probably the best-known and best-loved icon from the Eastern Orthodox Church. Ann Persson shares her journey of discovery through some of the historic and artistic traditions of icon-painting, including a midwinter pilgrimage to the Russian monastery for which Rublev's icon was originally commissioned. *The Circle of Love* is perfect introductory reading for all who are interested in exploring the use of icons in meditative prayer. *Endorsed by Sister Wendy Beckett.*

Seasons of the Spirit Teresa Morgan (£6.99)

Interspersing prose with poetry, this book is a journey through the seasons of the year and the high days and holy days of the Church. In the company of saints present and past, we travel from Advent Sunday to Advent Sunday, looking for the kingdom of heaven and reflecting on the many ways in which God's love reaches out to embrace and transform the world.

Quiet Spaces: Yesterday ed. Heather Fenton (£4.99)

With a new editor and a new format, *Quiet Spaces* explores 'Yesterday' from different perspectives, starting with the very beginnings of the universe. We also think about the psalmist as he considers his personal yesterday—his formation in the womb. Then we look back at our own 'yesterdays' and finally explore the Eucharist as encompassing past, present and future—which will lead us easily into the themes for the next two issues, 'Today' and 'Tomorrow'.

YOU CAN ORDER THE TITLES ON THESE TWO PAGES FROM CHRISTINA PRESS OR BRF, USING THE ORDER FORMS ON PAGES 140 AND 141.

Christina Press Publications Order Form

All of these publications are available from Christian bookshops everywhere or, in case of difficulty, direct from the publisher. Please make your selection below, complete the payment details and send your order with payment as appropriate to:

Christina Press Ltd, 17 Church Road, Tunbridge Wells, Kent TN1 1LG

		Qty	Price	Total
8700	God's Catalyst	___	£8.99	___
8701	Women Celebrating Faith	___	£5.99	___
8702	Precious to God	___	£5.99	___
8703	Angels Keep Watch	___	£5.99	___
8704	Life Path	___	£5.99	___
8705	Pathway Through Grief	___	£6.99	___
8706	Who'd Plant a Church?	___	£5.99	___
8707	Dear God, It's Me and It's Urgent	___	£6.99	___
8708	Not a Super-Saint	___	£6.99	___
8709	The Addiction of a Busy Life	___	£5.99	___
8710	In His Time	___	£5.99	___

POSTAGE AND PACKING CHARGES				
	UK	Europe	Surface	Air Mail
£7.00 & under	£1.25	£3.00	£3.50	£5.50
£7.10–£29.99	£2.25	£5.50	£6.50	£10.00
£30.00 & over	free	prices on request		

Total cost of books £ _____
Postage and Packing £ _____
TOTAL   £ _____

All prices are correct at time of going to press, are subject to the prevailing rate of VAT and may be subject to change without prior warning.

Name ____

Address ____

____

_________________________________ Postcode __________

Total enclosed £ _______ (cheques should be made payable to 'Christina Press Ltd')

☐ Please do not send me further information about Christina Press publications

BRF Publications Order Form

All of these publications are available from Christian bookshops everywhere, or in case of difficulty direct from the publisher. Please make your selection below, complete the payment details and send your order with payment as appropriate to:

BRF, 15 The Chambers, Vineyard, Abingdon OX14 3FE

		Qty	Price	Total
799 0	Growing a Caring Church	____	£6.99	____
750 1	The Circle of Love	____	£5.99	____
710 5	Seasons of the Spirit	____	£6.99	____
599 6	Quiet Spaces: Community	____	£4.99	____
600 9	Quiet Spaces: Nation	____	£4.99	____
659 7	Quiet Spaces: Yesterday	____	£4.99	____

POSTAGE AND PACKING CHARGES				
	UK	Europe	Surface	Air Mail
£7.00 & under	£1.25	£3.00	£3.50	£5.50
£7.10–£29.99	£2.25	£5.50	£6.50	£10.00
£30.00 & over	free	prices on request		

Total cost of books £ ________
Postage and Packing £ ________
TOTAL £ ________

All prices are correct at time of going to press, are subject to the prevailing rate of VAT and may be subject to change without prior warning.

Name ____

Address ____

_________________________________ Postcode ____________

Phone ________________ Email ____________________________

Total enclosed £ ________ (cheques should be made payable to 'BRF')

Please charge my Visa ❑ Mastercard ❑ Switch card ❑ with £ ________

Card no. ⬚⬚⬚⬚⬚⬚⬚⬚⬚⬚⬚⬚⬚⬚⬚⬚⬚⬚⬚

Expires ⬚⬚⬚⬚ Security code ⬚⬚⬚ Issue no (Switch) ⬚⬚⬚

Signature ____
(essential if paying by credit/Switch card)

❑ Please do not send me further information about BRF publications

Visit the BRF website at www.brf.org.uk

DBDWG0210

BRF is a Registered Charity

Subscription Information

Each issue of *Day by Day with God* is available from Christian bookshops everywhere. Copies may also be available through your church Book Agent or from the person who distributes Bible reading notes in your church.

Alternatively you may obtain *Day by Day with God* on subscription direct from the publishers. There are two kinds of subscription:

Individual Subscriptions are for four copies or less, and include postage and packing. To order an annual Individual Subscription please complete the details on page 144 and send the coupon with payment to BRF in Abingdon. You can also use the form to order a Gift Subscription for a friend.

Church Subscriptions are for five copies or more, sent to one address, and are supplied post free. Church Subscriptions run from 1 May to 30 April each year and are invoiced annually. To order a Church Subscription please complete the details opposite and send the coupon to BRF in Abingdon. You will receive an invoice with the first issue of notes.

All subscription enquiries should be directed to:

BRF
15 The Chambers
Vineyard
Abingdon
OX14 3FE

Tel: 01865 319700
Fax: 01865 319701
E-mail: subscriptions@brf.org.uk

Church Subscriptions

The Church Subscription rate for *Day by Day with God* will be £11.85 per person until April 2011.

❑ I would like to take out a church subscription for _______ (Qty) copies.

❑ Please start my order with the September 2010 / January / May 2011* issue. I would like to pay annually/receive an invoice with each edition of the notes*.
(*Please delete as appropriate)

Please do not send any money with your order. Send your order to BRF and we will send you an invoice. The Church Subscription year is from May to April. If you start subscribing in the middle of a subscription year we will invoice you for the remaining number of issues left in that year.

Name and address of the person organising the Church Subscription:

Name ____

Address ____

____

____

Postcode _______________ Telephone ____________________

Church ____

Name of Minister ____

Name and address of the person paying the invoice if the invoice needs to be sent directly to them:

Name ____

Address ____

____

Postcode _______________ Telephone ____________________

Please send your coupon to:

BRF
15 The Chambers
Vineyard
Abingdon
Oxon
OX14 3FE

❑ Please do not send me further information about BRF publications

DBDWG0210

BRF is a Registered Charity

Individual Subscriptions

❏ I would like to give a gift subscription (please complete both name and address sections below)

❏ I would like to take out a subscription myself (complete your name and address details only once)

Your name ____

Your address ____

_________________________________ Postcode _____________

Tel _________________ Email ________________________________

Gift subscription name ____________________________________

Gift subscription address _________________________________

_________________________________ Postcode _____________

Gift message (20 words max) _______________________________

____

Please send *Day by Day with God* for one year, beginning with the September 2010 / January / May 2011 issue: (delete as applicable)

	UK	Surface	Air Mail
Day by Day with God	❏ £14.85	❏ £16.65	❏ £19.65
2-year subscription	❏ £27.00	N/A	N/A
Day by Day with God + New Daylight by email	❏ £23.85	❏ £25.65	❏ £28.65

Please complete the payment details below and send your coupon, with appropriate payment, to BRF, 15 The Chambers, Vineyard, Abingdon, Oxon OX14 3FE

Total enclosed £ ______ (cheques should be made payable to 'BRF')

Please charge my Visa ❏ Mastercard ❏ Switch card ❏ with £ ________

Card no. ☐☐☐☐ ☐☐☐☐ ☐☐☐☐ ☐☐☐☐ ☐☐☐☐ ☐☐☐☐

Expires ☐☐☐☐ Security code ☐☐☐ Issue no (Switch) ☐☐☐☐

Signature ____
(essential if paying by credit/Switch card)

NB: These notes are also available from Christian bookshops everywhere.

❏ Please do not send me further information about BRF publications

DBDWG0210   BRF is a Registered Charity

144